FIREWALLS

THE ENGINEER'S GUIDE IN THE AGE OF CYBER THREATS

4 BOOKS IN 1

BOOK 1
FOUNDATIONS OF FIREWALL TECHNOLOGY: UNDERSTANDING CORE CONCEPTS, PROTOCOLS, AND ARCHITECTURES

BOOK 2
FIREWALL CONFIGURATION AND DEPLOYMENT: PRACTICAL GUIDES FOR ENGINEERS ON SETUP, RULES, AND OPTIMIZATION

BOOK 3
ADVANCED THREAT DETECTION AND RESPONSE: INTEGRATING FIREWALLS WITH MODERN SECURITY SYSTEMS

BOOK 4
NEXT-GEN FIREWALLS AND THE FUTURE OF NETWORK DEFENSE: AI, ZERO TRUST, AND EMERGING TECHNOLOGIES IN CYBERSECURITY

ROB BOTWRIGHT

Published by Rob Botwright
Library of Congress Cataloging-in-Publication Data
ISBN 978-1-83938-936-8
Cover design by Rizzo

Disclaimer

The contents of this book are based on extensive research and the best available historical sources. However, the author and publisher make no claims, promises, or guarantees about the accuracy, completeness, or adequacy of the information contained herein. The information in this book is provided on an "as is" basis, and the author and publisher disclaim any and all liability for any errors, omissions, or inaccuracies in the information or for any actions taken in reliance on such information. The opinions and views expressed in this book are those of the author and do not necessarily reflect the official policy or position of any organization or individual mentioned in this book. Any reference to specific people, places, or events is intended only to provide historical context and is not intended to defame or malign any group, individual, or entity. The information in this book is intended for educational and entertainment purposes only. It is not intended to be a substitute for professional advice or judgment. Readers are encouraged to conduct their own research and to seek professional advice where appropriate. Every effort has been made to obtain necessary permissions and acknowledgments for all images and other copyrighted material used in this book. Any errors or omissions in this regard are unintentional, and the author and publisher will correct them in future editions.

BOOK 1 - FOUNDATIONS OF FIREWALL TECHNOLOGY: UNDERSTANDING CORE CONCEPTS, PROTOCOLS, AND ARCHITECTURES

BOOK 1 - FOUNDATIONS OF FIREWALL TECHNOLOGY: UNDERSTANDING CORE CONCEPTS, PROTOCOLS, AND ARCHITECTURES

BOOK 1 - FOUNDATIONS OF FIREWALL TECHNOLOGY: UNDERSTANDING CORE CONCEPTS, PROTOCOLS, AND ARCHITECTURES

BOOK 1 - FOUNDATIONS OF FIREWALL TECHNOLOGY: UNDERSTANDING CORE CONCEPTS, PROTOCOLS, AND ARCHITECTURES

Introduction

In an era defined by rapid digital transformation, relentless cyber threats, and an ever-expanding attack surface, firewalls remain one of the most fundamental pillars of network security. Yet the role of the firewall has changed dramatically. No longer confined to static perimeter defense, firewalls today are expected to operate in cloud environments, protect distributed workforces, understand application behavior, and even contribute to real-time threat detection and automated response. For engineers and security professionals, this evolution presents both a challenge and an opportunity: to deepen their understanding of core technologies while mastering the tools and strategies needed to defend against modern threats.

Firewalls: The Engineer's Guide in the Age of Cyber Threats is a four-part technical series designed to provide a comprehensive and practical roadmap for professionals at every stage of their journey. Whether you're laying the groundwork for a secure network or exploring the leading edge of cybersecurity innovation, this series will help you navigate the complex intersection of networking, security, and systems engineering.

Book 1: Foundations of Firewall Technology explores the essential concepts that every engineer must understand—from the OSI model and TCP/IP stack to packet filtering, NAT, and firewall architectures. This foundational knowledge sets the stage for deeper, hands-on application in real-world environments.

Book 2: Firewall Configuration and Deployment serves as a detailed implementation guide, covering rule creation, segmentation strategies, traffic inspection, and optimization. It addresses both traditional deployment scenarios and modern architectures, offering proven methods to configure firewalls securely and effectively.

Book 3: Advanced Threat Detection and Response focuses on how firewalls integrate with broader security systems such as intrusion detection systems (IDS), SIEM platforms, endpoint detection and response (EDR), and automation frameworks. It explains how firewalls act as both sentinels and participants in coordinated defense strategies that require speed, intelligence, and adaptability.

Book 4: Next-Gen Firewalls and the Future of Network Defense examines the technologies reshaping the future of cybersecurity—artificial intelligence, Zero Trust models, SASE frameworks, and cloud-native architectures. It looks ahead to how firewalls are evolving into distributed, context-aware enforcement engines that secure users and data wherever they reside.

This series is written for engineers—not just to explain *what* firewalls do, but *why* they do it, *how* they're built, and *where* they're headed. The goal is not only to build secure configurations, but to cultivate a deeper understanding of the systems being protected, the threats being countered, and the architectures being designed.

Cybersecurity is no longer a specialized function; it is a shared responsibility embedded into the core of every network, every application, and every decision. Whether you're designing firewalls for enterprise networks, deploying them in cloud-native environments, or integrating them into automated threat response ecosystems, this guide is your companion for building smarter, stronger, and more adaptive defenses in the age of cyber threats.

BOOK 1
FOUNDATIONS OF FIREWALL TECHNOLOGY: UNDERSTANDING CORE CONCEPTS, PROTOCOLS, AND ARCHITECTURE

ROB BOTWRIGHT

Chapter 1: The Evolution of Network Security

The evolution of network security has been driven by the rapid expansion of digital infrastructure, the increasing sophistication of cyber threats, and the growing reliance on interconnected systems in every aspect of modern life. In the early days of computing, network security was almost an afterthought, primarily because networks were isolated, small-scale, and not accessible to the public. Most systems operated within trusted environments, and the biggest concerns revolved around physical access rather than remote attacks. As networks began to interconnect and the internet emerged, the need for securing communications and data became an undeniable priority.

In the 1980s and early 1990s, the concept of network security began to take shape, with basic packet-filtering firewalls and access control mechanisms being introduced to protect systems from unauthorized access. These early firewalls functioned by inspecting packet headers and determining whether traffic should be allowed based on simple rules like IP address, port number, and protocol type. At the time, this level of filtering was sufficient for many organizations, as threats were relatively unsophisticated and attacks were usually limited in scale and scope.

However, as the internet became widely accessible, the landscape of threats quickly evolved. Attackers began exploiting vulnerabilities in network protocols and software, leading to more aggressive and targeted campaigns. Worms, viruses, and distributed denial-of-service (DDoS) attacks became common, forcing organizations to implement stronger and more adaptive defenses. The introduction of stateful inspection firewalls marked a significant milestone during this period. These firewalls tracked the state of active connections and made decisions based on the context of traffic, rather than just static rules, allowing for more intelligent and dynamic filtering.

By the early 2000s, as web applications, email systems, and remote connectivity gained popularity, the attack surface expanded dramatically. This led to the rise of unified threat management (UTM) systems, which combined multiple security functions—such as firewalling, intrusion detection, antivirus, and content filtering—into a single platform. Organizations were now facing complex threats that required layered security strategies, and network security became an essential component of broader IT governance.

The mid-to-late 2000s also saw the proliferation of mobile devices, wireless networks, and cloud computing, all of which introduced new vectors for attack and redefined what needed to be protected. Traditional perimeter-based security models began to show their limitations. The idea that everything inside a network could be trusted was no longer viable, and this realization gave rise to more granular control mechanisms, identity-based access, and microsegmentation. Firewalls and security systems were now expected to operate not just at the network edge, but deep within the internal network infrastructure.

As cybercrime became more organized and financially motivated, threat actors started employing sophisticated tools and techniques to evade detection, including encryption, polymorphic malware, and social engineering. In response, security technologies evolved to include behavioral analysis, heuristics, and machine learning, enabling systems to detect and respond to previously unknown or zero-day threats. This period also marked the growing importance of threat intelligence sharing, as organizations recognized that no single entity could effectively combat the global scale of cyber threats alone.

With the shift toward cloud-first strategies and remote work, especially accelerated by global events in the 2020s, network security had to undergo another major transformation. The focus moved toward securing data and identities rather than just physical locations and devices. Concepts like Zero Trust Architecture emerged, advocating the principle of "never trust, always verify" for every user, device, and application, regardless of their location. At the same time, security operations became more reliant on automation, artificial intelligence, and real-time analytics to keep up with the volume and velocity of attacks.

Today's network security environment is defined by its complexity, agility, and the need for continuous adaptation. The security perimeter has effectively dissolved, replaced by dynamic trust models, cloud-native defenses, and globally distributed enforcement points. Firewalls are now just one piece of a much larger puzzle, integrated with broader security ecosystems that span endpoint protection, identity management, threat intelligence, and incident response. The evolution continues as emerging technologies like quantum computing, edge computing, and the Internet of Things present new challenges and opportunities for securing digital infrastructure.

Chapter 2: What Is a Firewall?

A firewall is a network security device or software that monitors, filters, and controls incoming and outgoing network traffic based on predetermined security rules. It acts as a barrier between a trusted internal network and untrusted external networks, such as the internet, with the goal of preventing unauthorized access while permitting legitimate communication. The fundamental purpose of a firewall is to enforce a security policy defined by the organization, allowing or blocking specific types of traffic according to criteria such as IP address, protocol, port number, application type, or user identity. Firewalls are one of the oldest and most essential components of network security, forming the backbone of perimeter defense strategies used to protect sensitive systems and data.

There are two main categories of firewalls: hardware firewalls and software firewalls. Hardware firewalls are physical appliances that are typically placed between the internet and the internal network. They offer robust performance and are commonly used in enterprise environments to protect large-scale networks. Software firewalls, on the other hand, are installed on individual computers or servers and are responsible for protecting a single device. These are especially useful for endpoint security and for situations where network segmentation or host-level control is required. In many cases, both hardware and software firewalls are used together to provide layered security and defense-in-depth.

The earliest firewalls operated using a method called packet filtering. These firewalls examined the headers of network packets and made decisions based on static rules. For example, a packet could be blocked if it came from a suspicious IP address or if it was using a disallowed port. While this method was fast and efficient, it lacked the ability to understand the context of connections and was vulnerable to spoofing and other basic evasion techniques. To address this limitation, stateful inspection firewalls were developed. These not only inspected individual packets but also tracked the state of active connections, enabling the firewall to make more informed decisions. Stateful firewalls could determine whether a packet was part of an existing, legitimate connection or if it was attempting to initiate an unauthorized session.

As applications and attacks became more complex, firewall technology evolved to include deeper levels of inspection. Application-layer firewalls, often referred to as proxy firewalls, operate at the highest level of the OSI model and can understand and filter traffic based on specific applications or services. This allows them to detect and block suspicious or non-compliant behavior that would pass undetected through lower-layer firewalls. For example, an application-layer firewall can analyze HTTP traffic to detect anomalies in web requests, such as cross-site scripting or SQL injection attempts. These firewalls often perform content inspection, malware scanning, and protocol validation, providing a more comprehensive level of control.

The development of Next-Generation Firewalls (NGFWs) marked a major leap forward in firewall technology. NGFWs combine traditional firewall features with advanced functionalities such as intrusion prevention systems (IPS), deep packet inspection, application awareness, user identity management, and integration with external threat intelligence services. They are designed to provide holistic protection in modern environments where threats are often embedded within legitimate-looking traffic. By analyzing traffic patterns, behaviors, and payloads, NGFWs can identify and stop threats that traditional firewalls might miss. These firewalls are also capable of decrypting and inspecting encrypted traffic, such as HTTPS, which has become increasingly common and poses a challenge for traditional security tools.

Firewalls are not limited to physical networks. With the rise of cloud computing and virtualized environments, cloud-native firewalls have become essential for protecting workloads in public and hybrid clouds. These firewalls are designed to operate within dynamic and distributed infrastructures, often using microsegmentation and software-defined networking principles to apply granular security policies across virtual machines, containers, and serverless functions. In addition to managing traffic flow, modern firewalls also collect and analyze vast amounts of telemetry, contributing to broader security analytics and incident response capabilities. Firewalls can be centrally managed through unified management consoles or security orchestration platforms, making them more scalable and easier to maintain in large environments. As part of an overall security architecture, firewalls work in conjunction with other tools such as endpoint protection, identity and access management, and threat intelligence systems to provide a comprehensive defense against cyber threats.

Chapter 3: Types of Firewalls

There are several types of firewalls, each designed to meet specific network security needs and architectural models, and understanding these types is essential for choosing the right firewall solution for any given environment. The most fundamental type is the **packet-filtering firewall**, which is one of the earliest and simplest forms of firewall technology. This type operates primarily at the network layer of the OSI model and examines packets in isolation, inspecting header information such as source and destination IP addresses, ports, and protocols. If a packet matches an allowed rule, it is permitted through; otherwise, it is dropped. While packet-filtering firewalls are fast and efficient, they do not maintain awareness of connection states and cannot detect more complex threats or malformed traffic, making them insufficient as a standalone defense in modern threat environments.

To address the limitations of packet filtering, **stateful inspection firewalls** were developed. These operate at both the network and transport layers and are capable of maintaining a state table that tracks active connections. By doing so, stateful firewalls understand the context of a session and can determine whether incoming packets are part of an existing, legitimate connection or an attempt to establish a new and potentially unauthorized one. This added intelligence allows for more granular control and better detection of suspicious or anomalous traffic patterns. Stateful inspection remains a core function in many firewalls today, though it is typically combined with more advanced features in enterprise-grade systems.

Another important category is the **proxy firewall**, also known as an application-layer firewall. This type acts as an intermediary between clients and the resources they wish to access, effectively terminating and re-establishing connections on behalf of the user. Because proxy firewalls operate at the application layer, they can inspect the actual contents of traffic, not just the metadata. For instance, an HTTP proxy firewall can analyze the structure of web requests, detect malicious payloads, and enforce application-specific rules. Proxy firewalls provide a high degree of visibility and control but often introduce latency and require more processing power, making them best suited for environments where security takes priority over speed.

With the growing complexity of threats and the increasing use of encrypted traffic and evasive techniques, **Next-Generation Firewalls (NGFWs)** have become the standard for modern network security. NGFWs incorporate the capabilities of packet filtering, stateful inspection, and deep packet inspection with additional features such as application awareness, user identity integration, intrusion prevention systems (IPS), and advanced threat detection. Unlike traditional firewalls that treat all traffic the same, NGFWs can distinguish between different types of applications, such as Skype, Dropbox, or YouTube, and apply policy rules accordingly. They can also correlate traffic patterns with known threat intelligence, enabling the identification of malicious behavior even if the traffic appears legitimate on the surface.

In virtualized and cloud environments, **virtual firewalls** or **cloud-native firewalls** have emerged as key players in securing dynamic infrastructure. These firewalls are software-based and designed to run in virtual machines, containers, or directly within cloud service provider environments. They offer flexible deployment options and can be integrated with orchestration tools to apply policies across hybrid or multi-cloud architectures. Virtual firewalls are especially important for securing east-west traffic, or traffic between workloads within the same data center or cloud environment, which often bypasses traditional perimeter defenses.

Host-based firewalls are another critical type, installed directly on individual endpoints or servers. These firewalls provide protection at the operating system level and are useful for enforcing policies on devices regardless of their network location. They are particularly effective in mobile or remote work scenarios where devices may frequently move between secure and insecure networks. Host-based firewalls can block unauthorized applications, filter traffic based on user-specific rules, and help contain threats before they spread across the network.

Another specialized category is the **network address translation (NAT) firewall**, which functions by masking internal IP addresses from external networks. While NAT is primarily a technique for conserving IP space and enabling multiple devices to share a single public IP, NAT firewalls also provide a layer of security by blocking unsolicited inbound traffic. When combined with stateful inspection, NAT firewalls can significantly reduce exposure to external threats by allowing only return traffic from initiated connections.

Firewalls can also be classified based on their **deployment location**, such as **perimeter firewalls**, which sit at the boundary between an organization's internal network and the internet, and **internal firewalls**, which segment internal networks for added security and traffic control. This segmentation is especially valuable in environments requiring regulatory compliance or zero trust architecture, where lateral movement within the network must be tightly controlled. Each type of firewall serves a unique role in a layered security strategy, and often, multiple types are used in conjunction to build a resilient defense.

Chapter 4: Firewall Architectures

Firewall architectures refer to the structural design and deployment strategies used to integrate firewalls within a network to maximize security, performance, and manageability. The architecture chosen depends on various factors, including the size of the organization, the complexity of the network, regulatory requirements, and the threat landscape. At the most basic level, a **single-layer firewall architecture** places a firewall at the perimeter of the network, acting as the primary gatekeeper between the internal network and the outside world. This traditional setup, often seen in small to medium-sized organizations, uses a single firewall to filter all incoming and outgoing traffic based on predefined security rules. While this approach is simple to manage and cost-effective, it provides limited segmentation and can become a single point of failure if the firewall is compromised.

As networks grew in complexity, the need for **multi-tiered firewall architectures** emerged. One of the most common of these is the **three-legged firewall architecture**, which uses three network interfaces: one for the internal network, one for the external or internet connection, and one for a **demilitarized**

zone (DMZ). The DMZ is a critical concept in firewall architecture, as it provides a buffer zone where public-facing services like web servers, mail servers, and DNS servers are hosted. By isolating these services from the internal network, the DMZ limits the impact of a potential breach. If an attacker compromises a system in the DMZ, they still face another layer of firewall protection before gaining access to sensitive internal resources.

Another widely used model is the **dual-firewall architecture**, where two separate firewalls are deployed—one between the internet and the DMZ, and another between the DMZ and the internal network. These firewalls may be from different vendors to reduce the risk of simultaneous exploitation due to shared vulnerabilities. This configuration offers a higher level of security by ensuring that even if one firewall is bypassed, a second, independently managed firewall stands in the way of internal systems. It also allows organizations to apply different security policies and inspection mechanisms at different points in the traffic flow.

In larger enterprises or highly regulated environments, **layered firewall architectures** are implemented to provide security through depth and segmentation. These architectures use multiple firewalls at different points within the network, often combined with network segmentation strategies. For example, different departments such as finance, human resources, and IT might each reside in separate network segments protected by internal firewalls. These internal firewalls enforce access controls between departments and contain potential breaches to isolated segments, preventing lateral movement by attackers. This approach is particularly important in zero trust environments, where no user or device is automatically trusted, even within the perimeter.

With the rise of virtualization and software-defined networking, **firewall architectures have evolved into cloud-based and virtualized models**. In a **cloud-native architecture**, firewalls are deployed as virtual appliances within public or private cloud environments. These firewalls can scale dynamically with workloads and integrate with cloud orchestration platforms, allowing for policy enforcement in distributed and ephemeral environments. Cloud-native firewalls support microsegmentation, where security policies are applied at the workload level, enabling fine-grained control over traffic between virtual machines, containers, or serverless applications.

Hybrid firewall architectures combine on-premises firewalls with cloud-based solutions, providing visibility and control across both environments. These setups are increasingly common in organizations that have adopted hybrid cloud strategies and require consistent policy enforcement across traditional and modern infrastructure. Hybrid models often rely on centralized management consoles to synchronize configurations, monitor traffic, and respond to threats across the entire network ecosystem. Such architectures enable flexibility and help maintain compliance in industries where data residency or sovereignty requirements prevent full cloud adoption.

Firewall architectures can also incorporate high availability (HA) and load balancing to ensure continuous protection and minimize downtime. In HA configurations, firewalls are deployed in active-passive or active-active clusters. In active-passive mode, one firewall handles all traffic while the other remains on standby, ready to take over in case of failure. In active-active setups, both firewalls process traffic simultaneously, offering better performance and fault tolerance. Load balancers can be used to distribute traffic evenly across multiple firewalls, preventing bottlenecks and improving response times. These features are essential for mission-critical environments where uptime and performance are as important as security.

As organizations adopt more agile and decentralized IT models, **decentralized firewall architectures** are also gaining traction. Instead of relying solely on perimeter-based firewalls, security is enforced closer to the endpoints and applications themselves. This approach aligns with zero trust principles and helps protect mobile users, IoT devices, and remote workers who operate outside the traditional network perimeter. Decentralized architectures often leverage a mix of host-based firewalls, endpoint detection and response (EDR), and identity-aware firewalls that make decisions based on user behavior and access context. The architectural choices made when deploying firewalls significantly influence an organization's security posture, operational efficiency, and resilience against cyber threats.

Chapter 5: Core Networking Protocols

Core networking protocols form the foundation of all digital communication, enabling devices, services, and applications to connect, interact, and exchange data across local and global networks. These protocols are essential for the operation of firewalls, as they define how information travels across the internet and within internal networks, and provide the parameters by which traffic can be inspected, filtered, or blocked. One of the most fundamental protocols is the **Internet Protocol (IP)**, which is responsible for addressing and routing packets of data from a source to a destination. Each device on a network is assigned an IP address, either IPv4 or IPv6, which serves as a unique identifier. IP is a connectionless protocol, meaning it does not establish a direct connection before sending data. Instead, it sends packets independently, and each may take a different route to reach the same destination.

Complementing IP is the **Transmission Control Protocol (TCP)**, which ensures reliable, ordered, and error-checked delivery of data between applications. TCP establishes a connection through a process known as the three-way handshake, which involves exchanging SYN, SYN-ACK, and ACK packets to confirm the readiness of both the sender and receiver. Once a connection is established, TCP ensures that packets arrive in sequence and without duplication. If any packets are lost or corrupted, TCP will retransmit them. Firewalls inspect TCP headers to enforce rules based on port numbers, sequence numbers, and connection states. For example, a firewall might allow outbound TCP traffic to port 443 for HTTPS connections but deny inbound connections to port 23, which is associated with the unsecure Telnet protocol.

Another widely used transport layer protocol is the **User Datagram Protocol (UDP)**, which, unlike TCP, does not provide guaranteed delivery, ordering, or error checking. UDP is a lightweight protocol often used in time-sensitive applications such as video streaming, VoIP, online gaming, and DNS queries, where speed is more critical than reliability. Because UDP lacks connection management, it is more difficult for firewalls to track the state of a communication session, which can introduce challenges in applying precise security controls. Firewalls often need to inspect the application layer content of UDP packets to make more informed decisions about whether to allow or block traffic.

The **Internet Control Message Protocol (ICMP)** plays a different role in network communication by enabling diagnostic functions and error reporting. ICMP is commonly used by tools such as ping and traceroute to check the availability and responsiveness of network devices. It can report issues such as unreachable hosts, time exceeded in transit, or problems with packet fragmentation. While ICMP is valuable for network troubleshooting, it can also be misused in reconnaissance attacks, prompting many firewalls to restrict or rate-limit ICMP traffic to prevent abuse while still allowing necessary diagnostic operations.

At the application layer, protocols such as **HTTP**, **HTTPS**, **FTP**, **DNS**, and **SMTP** come into play. Firewalls often use these protocols to define rule sets that distinguish between safe and potentially dangerous traffic. **HTTP** and **HTTPS**, which are used for web browsing, operate on ports 80 and 443 respectively, and are closely monitored due to their prevalence and the frequency with which attackers exploit web-based vulnerabilities. HTTPS encrypts the data exchanged between a client and a server, providing confidentiality and integrity, but it also poses challenges for security tools like firewalls, which must implement SSL/TLS inspection capabilities to examine the contents of encrypted traffic.

Domain Name System (DNS) is another critical protocol that translates human-readable domain names into IP addresses. Firewalls may inspect DNS queries to detect access to malicious domains or to enforce content filtering policies. However, attackers may use techniques such as DNS tunneling to bypass traditional security measures, prompting advanced firewalls to analyze DNS traffic more deeply. **Simple Mail Transfer Protocol (SMTP)**, used for sending emails, and **Post Office Protocol (POP3)** or **IMAP**, used for receiving them, are also frequent targets of spam and phishing campaigns, making them important points of inspection for firewalls in corporate environments.

Understanding these core protocols is essential for configuring firewall rules effectively. Each protocol behaves differently, and firewalls must be able to interpret their unique characteristics to ensure accurate filtering. For example, stateful firewalls need to understand TCP's session establishment and teardown processes, while application-aware firewalls may parse HTTP headers to identify suspicious behavior. In modern environments, where traffic can be highly dynamic and often encrypted, awareness of how these core protocols operate allows network engineers to create security policies that strike the right balance between protection, usability, and performance. Firewalls, intrusion detection systems, and other security tools rely on the consistent structure and behavior of these protocols to recognize patterns, identify anomalies, and enforce access control at multiple layers of the OSI model.

Chapter 6: Zones, Interfaces, and Segmentation

Zones, interfaces, and segmentation are fundamental concepts in firewall design and network architecture, playing a critical role in how traffic is managed, isolated, and secured across different parts of a network. At the most basic level, an **interface** is a point of connection between a firewall and a specific segment of the network, such as a local area network (LAN), a wide area network (WAN), or a demilitarized zone (DMZ). Each interface can be assigned an IP address and configured with various security policies. Interfaces serve as the physical or virtual pathways through which data enters and exits the firewall, and their configuration directly affects how traffic is evaluated and controlled.

Zones are logical groupings of interfaces that represent different trust levels or network purposes. For example, a common firewall configuration might include a **trusted zone** for internal corporate systems, an **untrusted zone** for internet-facing traffic, and a **DMZ** for public-facing services such as web servers or email gateways. Zones allow administrators to apply security policies based on the trust relationship between different parts of the network, rather than managing rules for individual interfaces. This abstraction simplifies policy management and ensures consistency when the same level of security is needed across multiple interfaces. Traffic moving between zones is subject to inspection, filtering, and logging based on defined security policies, while traffic within a zone is typically allowed to pass more freely, although internal segmentation is increasingly common even within trusted environments.

Segmentation refers to the practice of dividing a network into smaller parts, or segments, each of which can be individually managed and secured. There are different types of segmentation, including physical, virtual, and logical segmentation. **Physical segmentation** uses separate hardware and cabling for different parts of the network, offering strong isolation but limited scalability. **Virtual segmentation**, often implemented through VLANs (Virtual Local Area Networks), allows multiple segmented networks to share the same physical infrastructure while maintaining logical separation. **Logical segmentation**, which may be implemented through firewall zones or routing policies, provides flexible control over traffic flow based on user roles, applications, or device types.

Firewalls play a central role in enforcing segmentation by inspecting and filtering traffic that crosses from one segment to another. In a flat network with little to no segmentation, any compromised device can potentially access the entire network, making lateral movement by attackers easier. When networks are properly segmented, each segment becomes a security boundary that limits the spread of malware, reduces the risk of data breaches, and improves overall visibility and control. Firewalls can enforce **access control lists (ACLs)**, **network address translation (NAT)**, and **intrusion prevention rules** at each segment boundary, ensuring that only legitimate and authorized communication is allowed between zones.

A well-designed segmentation strategy often includes a **DMZ**, which acts as a buffer zone between internal and external networks. Systems placed in the DMZ are accessible from the internet but are isolated from the internal network. This reduces the risk of external attackers using publicly exposed services as a stepping stone to internal resources. Firewalls between the DMZ and the internal network typically enforce strict controls, allowing only specific, necessary traffic to pass, such as web application traffic to a backend database.

In more advanced architectures, **microsegmentation** is used to apply security policies at a very granular level, often down to individual workloads, applications, or users. This is common in data centers and cloud environments where traditional perimeter defenses are insufficient. Microsegmentation is typically enforced through software-defined networking (SDN) and next-generation firewalls that can identify and control traffic based on application behavior and user identity. By using fine-grained segmentation, organizations can ensure that even if one part of the network is compromised, the attacker cannot easily move to other parts of the environment.

Proper configuration of zones and interfaces is essential for the effectiveness of segmentation strategies. Misconfigurations can lead to security holes, such as open pathways between high-trust and low-trust zones, or overly permissive rules that defeat the purpose of segmentation. Security teams must carefully design and maintain their firewall architectures to ensure that interfaces are correctly mapped to zones, and that rules governing inter-zone communication are aligned with the organization's security policies and compliance requirements. Logging and monitoring should also be implemented to track traffic flows between zones and detect any anomalies or violations of expected behavior. In combination, zones, interfaces, and segmentation enable organizations to build layered, resilient defenses that support both security and operational flexibility.

Chapter 7: Access Control and Rule Logic

Access control and rule logic are at the core of firewall functionality, defining how traffic is evaluated, permitted, or denied based on a set of preconfigured security policies. Firewalls act as enforcement points for access control, interpreting the rules created by administrators to determine whether a given network packet should be allowed to pass through or be blocked. Access control is the mechanism that defines who or what is allowed to access specific resources, while rule logic determines how these access decisions are executed by the firewall engine. These two concepts work together to ensure that only authorized traffic is allowed into or out of a network, reducing the attack surface and maintaining compliance with organizational security standards.

The most basic form of access control in a firewall environment involves matching traffic against a rule set that considers elements such as source IP address, destination IP address, source and destination ports, and the protocol used, such as TCP, UDP, or ICMP. Each rule typically includes an action, either "allow" or "deny," and conditions under which that action should be applied. For example, a rule might allow HTTP traffic from a specific internal subnet to any external IP address, but deny all incoming traffic to that same subnet unless it is part of an established connection. These rules are read from top to bottom in a linear or hierarchical fashion, meaning the first rule that matches the traffic criteria is the one that gets enforced. This order of operations is crucial and must be carefully planned to avoid unintended access.

Modern firewalls often expand this logic to include additional layers of control such as time-based rules, user identity, device type, application signature, or even behavioral indicators. This allows for more granular policies like permitting file transfers only during business hours, allowing access to an internal database only from a specific set of devices managed by the IT department, or blocking social media applications during work hours. Such functionality is typically seen in next-generation firewalls (NGFWs), which operate beyond traditional network-layer rules and introduce deep packet inspection and contextual awareness into access control decisions.

A key aspect of rule logic is the concept of the implicit deny, which is a hidden rule found at the end of most firewall rule sets. If none of the explicit rules match a packet, the firewall automatically drops or rejects it by default. This implicit deny is a best practice that ensures only explicitly permitted traffic can pass, reducing the chance of unauthorized access caused by overlooked or missing rules. However, administrators must always be aware of the existence of this rule to avoid confusion when legitimate traffic appears to be blocked without an obvious cause in the visible rule set.

Another important consideration is rule optimization. Over time, firewall rule sets can become cluttered with outdated, redundant, or conflicting entries, especially in large environments where multiple administrators are making changes. A poorly maintained rule base can slow down firewall performance, introduce security gaps, and make troubleshooting difficult. Regular reviews and cleanup of firewall rules are necessary to maintain efficiency and clarity. Firewalls that support rule hit counters and logging can help identify which rules are actively being used and which ones are no longer relevant.

Firewalls may also support access control through policy objects, which allow administrators to abstract and group common elements like IP addresses, port ranges, or users into reusable components. This approach simplifies rule creation and ensures consistency across different parts of the configuration. For example, instead of writing separate rules for each IP address belonging to the finance department, an administrator could define a single "Finance_Network" object and reference it throughout the rule base.

In distributed or cloud-based environments, centralized access control and policy orchestration become even more critical. With multiple firewalls deployed across different regions or virtual networks, consistent rule logic must be applied to avoid discrepancies and maintain uniform protection. Centralized management tools allow for the creation, deployment, and auditing of rules across the infrastructure, reducing the chances of misconfiguration and improving visibility into access patterns. Furthermore, automated policy management systems can dynamically adjust rules in response to changing conditions, such as detecting a compromised device and automatically restricting its access to sensitive network zones.

Rule logic also extends to the use of logging and alerting mechanisms. Each access control decision made by the firewall can be logged, creating an audit trail that is invaluable for both security monitoring and forensic analysis. Alerts can be triggered when rules are violated or when attempts are made to access forbidden resources, allowing security teams to react in real time to potential threats. Together, access control and rule logic provide a flexible yet powerful way to shape traffic flow, enforce security policies, and protect critical assets in increasingly complex network environments.

Chapter 8: NAT, PAT, and Port Forwarding

NAT, PAT, and port forwarding are essential technologies in network security and firewall configuration, enabling organizations to manage IP address allocation, conserve public IP space, and securely expose internal services to external networks. **Network Address Translation (NAT)** is a technique used to translate private IP addresses used inside a network to public IP addresses that can be routed across the internet. This translation happens at the network edge, typically on a router or firewall, and allows multiple devices within a private network to access external resources while appearing as a single public IP address to the outside world. NAT provides both functional and security benefits by hiding internal IP addresses, which are not directly reachable from the internet, thereby reducing exposure to external threats.

There are several variations of NAT, but the most common and widely used is **Port Address Translation (PAT)**, also known as **NAT overload**. PAT allows many internal devices to share a single public IP address by assigning unique port numbers to each session. When a device inside the network initiates a connection to an external server, the firewall or NAT device modifies the source IP address to the public IP and assigns a unique source port number. This combination of public IP and port allows the device to track multiple simultaneous connections from different internal hosts, ensuring that return traffic is correctly delivered to the original sender. For example, if three devices on a local network access a website, they might all appear to the web server as coming from the same public IP, but with different source ports. The NAT device keeps a translation table that maps each port to the correct internal IP and port, allowing for proper routing of response traffic.

Static NAT, another form of NAT, maps one internal IP address to one public IP address. This is useful when a specific internal resource, such as a server, needs to be consistently reachable from the internet using a dedicated public IP. However, due to the limited availability of IPv4 addresses, static NAT is often used sparingly and only for high-priority services. **Dynamic NAT**, in contrast, maps private IPs to public IPs from a pool on a first-come, first-served basis, without reusing public IPs with port multiplexing like PAT does. Although dynamic NAT provides address conservation, it does not support as many simultaneous connections as PAT, making it less common in modern networks.

Port forwarding is a specific application of NAT that enables external users to access services hosted on internal network devices. It works by forwarding traffic from a specific port on the public IP address to a designated port and IP address within the private network. For instance, if a company hosts a web server on an internal IP address, the firewall can be configured to forward all incoming traffic on TCP port 80 to that server's internal IP and port. This setup allows the server to be accessible from the internet without assigning it a public IP address. Port forwarding is widely used for services like web servers, email servers, remote desktop access, and gaming servers. However, it must be configured carefully to prevent exposing vulnerable services or creating security holes in the network.

Firewalls play a critical role in managing and enforcing NAT, PAT, and port forwarding rules. Administrators define policies that determine which traffic is translated, how addresses are mapped, and which internal systems are accessible from the outside. Misconfigurations can lead to unintended exposure, such as leaving internal systems open to unauthorized access or allowing malicious traffic to bypass security controls. To reduce risk, it's common practice to restrict forwarded ports to specific external IP addresses, apply intrusion prevention rules to the forwarded traffic, and monitor logs for unusual access patterns. Many firewalls also support **reflexive NAT** or **bidirectional NAT**, which dynamically create return rules when outbound connections are initiated, further streamlining secure communication.

In IPv6 networks, NAT is generally not required due to the vast address space available, allowing every device to have a globally unique IP. However, many organizations still use NAT in IPv6 deployments for policy enforcement, address management, or compatibility with legacy systems. Despite debates around its necessity in modern protocols, NAT and its variants remain central to how organizations design secure, scalable, and functional network environments. Firewalls that support advanced NAT features offer greater flexibility and control over traffic flows, enabling network architects to create efficient topologies that balance accessibility with protection.

Chapter 9: Logging and Monitoring Essentials

Logging and monitoring are essential components of any firewall deployment, providing visibility into network activity, detecting anomalies, and supporting both proactive and reactive security operations. Without logging, firewall rules operate in a vacuum, silently allowing or denying traffic with no record of what occurred. With proper logging, every packet or connection that passes through the firewall can be documented, including details such as source and destination IP addresses, ports, protocols, timestamps, rule matches, and whether the traffic was allowed or blocked. This data becomes the foundation for monitoring, analysis, and decision-making, enabling administrators to understand usage patterns, troubleshoot connectivity issues, and detect signs of malicious behavior or policy violations.

Firewall logs are typically categorized into several types, including traffic logs, event logs, threat logs, system logs, and configuration logs. **Traffic logs** capture information about allowed or denied connections, including session start and end times, byte counts, and flags that indicate whether the connection was normal or suspicious. These logs are especially valuable for identifying unusual patterns such as repeated connection attempts to closed ports, port scanning behavior, or large data transfers that might indicate exfiltration. **Event logs** focus on changes in the firewall's operational state, such as service restarts, link failures, or high CPU usage, and can provide early warnings of system instability or tampering. **Threat logs** document events related to intrusion prevention systems, malware detection, and other security services that are often integrated into next-generation firewalls. They provide critical information about attack types, signatures triggered, severity levels, and mitigation actions taken. **System logs** capture messages from the operating system or firmware, helping administrators maintain the health and performance of the device. **Configuration logs** record all changes made to firewall settings, including rule modifications, user actions, and firmware updates, allowing for accountability and rollback in case of errors or unauthorized changes.

To make use of these logs, organizations must implement effective **monitoring practices**, which involve collecting, aggregating, analyzing, and acting upon logged data. Monitoring can be done manually, but due to the high volume of data generated, most organizations rely on centralized log management systems or **Security Information**

and Event Management (SIEM) platforms. These systems normalize log formats from multiple sources, correlate events across the network, and apply logic to detect complex attack patterns or compliance violations. For example, a SIEM might detect a brute-force login attempt by correlating failed authentication events across multiple systems, even if each individual system did not flag the activity as suspicious on its own.

A key principle in firewall logging is to **log both allowed and denied traffic**, as focusing solely on blocked connections can give a false sense of security. Allowed traffic can also be malicious, especially if a compromised internal device is communicating with a command-and-control server or leaking sensitive data. Monitoring outbound traffic is just as important as monitoring inbound traffic, since attackers often try to establish outbound connections to maintain persistence or extract information. By analyzing patterns in allowed traffic, such as unexpected destinations, new protocols, or abnormal timing, administrators can uncover stealthy threats that might otherwise go unnoticed.

Alerting mechanisms are an important extension of monitoring, enabling real-time responses to critical events. Firewalls can be configured to trigger alerts based on defined thresholds or conditions, such as a high number of denied connections from the same IP, attempts to access restricted services, or detections of known malware signatures. Alerts can be sent via email, SMS, or integrated with automated response systems that take immediate action, such as blocking an offending IP or isolating a device from the network. While alerts are valuable, they must be carefully tuned to avoid false positives and alert fatigue, which can cause important warnings to be missed.

Retention policies for logs also play a vital role in monitoring and forensic analysis. Security incidents are not always detected immediately, so it is important to retain logs for a sufficient period to allow for retrospective investigations. The exact retention period depends on regulatory requirements, storage capacity, and organizational policy, but many standards recommend keeping security logs for at least one year. Logs must be protected from tampering, with access controls and integrity checks in place to ensure their reliability. Encryption, digital signatures, and secure storage are often used to preserve the authenticity of log data.

Regular review and analysis of logs and monitoring data helps organizations refine firewall rules, detect configuration errors, and adapt to evolving threats. Dashboards, visualizations, and scheduled reports can highlight trends, top talkers, blocked threats, and other key metrics. This visibility supports continuous improvement and strengthens the overall security posture of the network. In environments with compliance obligations, logs and monitoring reports also serve as evidence of due diligence and control enforcement, satisfying auditors and regulators. Firewalls that support comprehensive logging and robust monitoring integration empower security teams to move from reactive defense to informed, proactive protection.

Chapter 10: Limitations and Common Misconceptions

Firewalls are an essential part of modern network security, but they are not without limitations, and many misconceptions persist about what firewalls can and cannot do. One of the most common misunderstandings is the belief that installing a firewall alone is enough to secure a network. While firewalls play a critical role in enforcing access control and filtering traffic, they do not provide protection against all types of threats. For example, a firewall cannot stop malware that is introduced through infected USB drives, nor can it detect social engineering attacks like phishing emails that trick users into revealing credentials or installing malicious software. Firewalls also cannot protect against insider threats when a legitimate user with access intentionally or unintentionally causes harm. These scenarios fall outside the scope of what a firewall is designed to do, and relying solely on firewall protection can create a dangerous sense of security.

Another limitation is that firewalls are only as effective as the rules and configurations they are given. Poorly designed rule sets, overly permissive policies, or misconfigurations can leave gaps that attackers can exploit. For instance, if an administrator allows unrestricted outbound traffic, malware installed on a compromised device may be able to exfiltrate data without triggering any firewall alerts. Similarly, excessive exceptions in firewall rules can render the entire policy ineffective by allowing too much trust in traffic that should be scrutinized. Even the best firewall technology cannot compensate for human error or a lack of oversight in its deployment and maintenance.

A widespread misconception is that firewalls can fully inspect encrypted traffic by default. In reality, inspecting encrypted traffic such as HTTPS or SSL/TLS requires additional capabilities like SSL decryption, which must be explicitly enabled and configured. Without decryption, the firewall can only see the metadata of the traffic—such as IP addresses and ports—but not the actual payload. This limits its ability to detect threats hidden within encrypted sessions, which are increasingly used by attackers to bypass traditional security tools. However, enabling SSL inspection introduces its own challenges, including privacy concerns, performance overhead, and the complexity of certificate management. Organizations must weigh these trade-offs carefully when deciding how deeply to inspect encrypted traffic.

Another limitation arises from the evolving nature of modern networks. Firewalls were originally designed to secure a clear network perimeter, but with the rise of remote work, mobile devices, cloud computing, and hybrid environments, the traditional perimeter has become blurred or nonexistent. Traffic now flows across various platforms and infrastructures, often beyond the visibility of a single firewall. In such cases, relying on a perimeter-based firewall architecture alone is inadequate, and additional controls such as endpoint protection, cloud-native firewalls, and identity-based access systems are needed to provide comprehensive coverage. The misconception that the firewall still serves as the sole gatekeeper can lead to critical blind spots in these decentralized environments.

It is also important to recognize that firewalls are not immune to being targeted themselves. Like any other network device, firewalls can have software vulnerabilities, firmware bugs, or insecure default settings that attackers can exploit. If a firewall is not regularly patched or monitored, it may become a weak link in the security chain rather than a safeguard. Attackers may also attempt to flood the firewall with traffic in a denial-of-service attack to exhaust its resources and create a window for intrusion. This makes it essential to include firewalls in the broader patch management and monitoring processes alongside other infrastructure components.

Another common misunderstanding is assuming that all traffic passing through a firewall is automatically logged and analyzed. While most firewalls are capable of generating extensive logs, logging must be explicitly configured, and storage must be provisioned to handle the volume of data. In many cases, organizations only log denied traffic or select categories of events due to resource constraints, missing valuable insights about allowed traffic that may be indicative of an ongoing attack. Without comprehensive logging and centralized monitoring, the visibility provided by firewalls is limited and reactive rather than proactive.

Finally, some believe that firewalls can distinguish between legitimate and malicious traffic purely based on ports and IP addresses. While this was true for older generation firewalls, modern threats often use standard ports and legitimate-looking traffic patterns to evade detection. Application-layer firewalls and next-generation features have improved this capability, but they still depend on accurate identification, rule tuning, and integration with threat intelligence sources. Even the most advanced firewall technologies require constant updating, maintenance, and contextual awareness to remain effective in a threat landscape that is constantly changing. Understanding these limitations and misconceptions helps set realistic expectations and reinforces the need for a multi-layered approach to network security.

BOOK 2
FIREWALL CONFIGURATION AND DEPLOYMENT:
PRACTICAL GUIDES FOR ENGINEERS ON SETUP,
RULES, AND OPTIMIZATION

ROB BOTWRIGHT

Chapter 1: Preparing for Deployment

Preparing for deployment is a critical phase in the implementation of any firewall solution, as it lays the groundwork for a secure, efficient, and effective network defense strategy. This stage involves much more than simply selecting a firewall appliance or software—it requires a thorough understanding of the network environment, identification of security requirements, coordination with stakeholders, and the development of clear, actionable deployment plans. Before any hardware is installed or any configuration begins, a comprehensive assessment of the existing network architecture must be conducted. This includes mapping out current traffic flows, identifying trusted and untrusted zones, understanding which applications and services are in use, and determining how users access internal and external resources.

A key step in preparing for deployment is defining the **security objectives** and **risk tolerance** of the organization. This involves asking what needs to be protected, from whom, and under what conditions. Whether the primary goal is regulatory compliance, data protection, or service availability, these objectives will influence the type of firewall chosen, the rules that are applied, and the placement of the firewall within the network. During this stage, it is important to consult with various departments—such as IT operations, security, compliance, and business units—to gather input and ensure that the deployment aligns with both technical and organizational priorities.

Once the objectives are clear, a **detailed inventory** of assets should be created. This includes servers, workstations, networking equipment, applications, and data repositories, along with their respective IP addresses, operating systems, and roles in the environment. This inventory will help define what traffic is legitimate and what should be blocked, as well as assist in creating precise access control policies. At the same time, it is necessary to document the existing security controls in place, such as intrusion prevention systems, antivirus solutions, endpoint protection, or cloud access gateways, to ensure that the firewall is deployed as part of a cohesive security architecture rather than in isolation.

Another essential part of preparing for deployment is determining **firewall placement**. This decision depends on the network's topology and the desired level of visibility and control. Firewalls can be deployed at the network perimeter, between different internal segments, in front of critical assets, or in cloud environments. In many cases, a combination of placements is used to create a layered defense. For example, a perimeter firewall may filter traffic entering from the internet, while internal firewalls enforce segmentation between departments or applications. Proper placement ensures that the firewall can inspect and filter traffic effectively without becoming a bottleneck or leaving parts of the network exposed.

Capacity planning is also important to ensure that the chosen firewall can handle the expected volume of traffic without degrading performance. This includes evaluating metrics such as throughput, number of concurrent sessions, latency, and VPN connections. Underestimating these requirements can lead to performance issues or failures under load. Firewall vendors typically provide performance specifications for their devices, but real-world performance can vary depending on enabled features such as deep packet inspection, intrusion prevention, or SSL decryption, all of which consume processing resources. A realistic evaluation of current and future traffic demands will help avoid capacity-related problems post-deployment.

The next step involves preparing a **policy framework** that outlines the intended rule sets, access controls, and security zones. Policies should be aligned with the principle of least privilege, allowing only the minimum necessary access between users, systems, and services. Starting with a baseline policy that denies all traffic by default and selectively allowing required traffic can minimize risk and simplify auditing. This is also the time to identify high-risk services, such as remote desktop, file sharing, or legacy protocols, and determine whether they should be restricted, monitored, or replaced with more secure alternatives.

Before going live, it is critical to plan for **testing and validation** of the firewall configuration. This includes simulating both normal and abnormal traffic to ensure that the firewall enforces policies as expected, does not block legitimate business functions, and generates appropriate logs and alerts. A lab environment or test network can be used for initial validation before deployment into production. Proper documentation of all configurations, policies, and procedures is essential for maintenance, troubleshooting, and future audits. Training for IT staff should also be included in the preparation phase so that those responsible for operating the firewall are fully familiar with its interface, features, and management tools.

Chapter 2: Choosing the Right Firewall Solution

Choosing the right firewall solution is one of the most important decisions in the design and implementation of a secure network infrastructure. This process involves evaluating not only the features and capabilities of available firewall technologies but also the specific needs and operational context of the organization. Every environment has unique security, performance, compliance, and scalability requirements, and selecting a firewall without carefully considering these factors can lead to gaps in protection, operational inefficiencies, or unnecessary costs. The first step in choosing the right solution is to clearly define the goals of the deployment, which may include preventing unauthorized access, enabling secure remote connectivity, enforcing compliance with regulatory standards, segmenting internal network zones, or inspecting encrypted traffic for advanced threats.

There are different types of firewall solutions available, each suited to different environments. Traditional hardware-based firewalls are ideal for protecting physical data centers or campus networks, providing high throughput and robust perimeter protection. These appliances often include multiple network interfaces, dedicated processing power, and advanced features such as high availability and failover. On the other hand, software-based firewalls may be better suited for individual endpoints, virtual environments, or small branch offices where deploying dedicated hardware may not be feasible. Virtual firewalls, which operate within hypervisors or cloud platforms, are essential in modern environments where workloads are no longer bound to physical infrastructure. These virtual instances offer the same features as physical appliances but provide more flexibility in terms of deployment and scalability, especially in hybrid or multi-cloud architectures.

When evaluating firewall solutions, one of the most critical criteria is **feature set and functionality**. Basic firewall capabilities include packet filtering, access control lists, and stateful inspection. However, modern networks require more advanced capabilities such as application-layer filtering, intrusion prevention systems (IPS), deep packet inspection (DPI), secure web gateways, SSL/TLS decryption, and integration with external threat intelligence feeds. A next-generation firewall (NGFW) typically includes these capabilities and adds the ability to identify applications and users, enforce identity-based policies, and detect threats in real-time. If an organization requires granular control over web applications, support for encrypted traffic inspection, or integration with active directory services, then selecting a next-generation solution is often the appropriate choice.

Another essential consideration is **performance**. The firewall must be capable of handling the expected network throughput without becoming a bottleneck. Performance metrics such as maximum throughput, number of concurrent sessions, new sessions per second, and latency under load are critical for assessing whether a firewall can meet the demands of the environment. These values can vary significantly depending on the enabled features. For example, turning on SSL decryption or intrusion prevention can reduce the maximum throughput, so it is important to evaluate the firewall's real-world performance with all required features enabled. If the firewall will be deployed in a high-traffic environment such as a data center, the performance specifications must exceed the anticipated load to maintain network stability and avoid degraded user experience.

Ease of management and **visibility** are also key factors in the selection process. A firewall that is difficult to configure, manage, or monitor will lead to administrative overhead and potential misconfigurations. Solutions with centralized management consoles, graphical policy editors, role-based access control, and detailed reporting tools provide a more manageable and scalable framework. Logging, alerting, and integration with Security Information and Event Management (SIEM) platforms are critical for ongoing monitoring, incident response, and compliance auditing. Some solutions also offer automation features, allowing for dynamic policy updates based on threat intelligence or behavioral analysis, which can significantly enhance response time to emerging threats.

Vendor reputation, support, and licensing model must also be evaluated. Working with a vendor that offers reliable technical support, regular updates, and a clear upgrade path is essential for maintaining long-term security and performance. Licensing models vary between vendors, with some charging per user, per device, or based on feature sets. Careful analysis of the total cost of ownership, including initial purchase, subscriptions, and ongoing maintenance, ensures that the selected firewall solution aligns with both the budget and strategic goals of the organization. Choosing the right firewall is not a one-size-fits-all decision, and a thoughtful, criteria-driven approach will help ensure the solution provides effective protection and operational value.

Chapter 3: Initial Setup and Network Integration

Initial setup and network integration are crucial phases in deploying a firewall and ensuring that it functions correctly within the broader IT environment. This process begins with the physical or virtual installation of the firewall device, which includes powering it on, connecting it to the appropriate network segments, and ensuring console or remote access for configuration. Whether the firewall is hardware-based or virtual, the initial setup typically involves assigning management IP addresses, configuring administrative access credentials, and verifying connectivity to ensure that the device can be managed securely over the network. It is common practice to perform these initial tasks in a controlled environment, such as a staging area or lab, before deploying the firewall into production, allowing administrators to verify configurations and reduce the risk of errors impacting business operations.

Once basic connectivity is established, the next step is to define **interface roles and security zones**. Each network interface on the firewall must be mapped to a logical security zone, such as internal, external, DMZ, or guest. These zones represent different trust levels and help enforce segmentation by controlling how traffic is allowed to move between them. The firewall should be configured to default to a "deny all" policy between zones, allowing traffic only where explicitly permitted. This approach supports the principle of least privilege and ensures that only the minimum necessary communication is allowed. Defining the IP addressing scheme, subnet masks, and gateway relationships for each interface is also part of this step, and it requires careful alignment with the existing network architecture to avoid IP conflicts or routing loops.

Routing configuration is a fundamental part of network integration, as the firewall must know how to reach all other parts of the network and direct traffic appropriately. Static routes may be used for simple or smaller networks, while larger environments typically rely on dynamic routing protocols such as OSPF or BGP to allow the firewall to learn routes automatically and adapt to changes in network topology. Firewalls must be integrated into the network in such a way that they can inspect traffic between internal segments, to and from the internet, and across VPN tunnels if applicable. It is also necessary to ensure that any existing network address translation (NAT) policies are compatible with the firewall's routing logic, as mismatches can result in broken connections or unanticipated exposure.

Policy definition is the core of firewall setup, involving the creation of rules that govern which traffic is allowed or denied based on source, destination, port, protocol, user, and application. During initial setup, it is common to define a baseline set of policies to enable essential business services while logging all other traffic for analysis. These rules are created within the context of the security zones and must be carefully ordered to ensure that the firewall enforces them correctly. Rule order is significant because firewalls typically evaluate rules from top to bottom and stop at the first match. Logging should be enabled for both allowed and denied traffic, providing valuable visibility during the initial testing and tuning phase.

Integration with existing infrastructure is also a critical task during setup. This includes linking the firewall with directory services such as Active Directory for identity-based policies, configuring logging to forward events to a centralized SIEM system, and enabling alerting for specific rule matches or anomalies. If the firewall includes intrusion prevention, antivirus scanning, or application control modules, these features should be activated and tuned according to the organization's risk profile. For environments using remote access or site-to-site VPNs, initial setup also involves configuring encryption settings, tunnel endpoints, authentication mechanisms, and failover behavior.

Testing and validation are essential parts of the setup process, ensuring that the firewall does not inadvertently block critical services or allow unwanted traffic. This involves simulating both normal user behavior and potential attack scenarios to confirm that policies are working as intended. Tools such as packet capture utilities, traceroute, and connection tests can assist in diagnosing routing and access issues. During testing, administrators should review firewall logs in real-time to identify misconfigurations or unexpected behavior and make adjustments as necessary. Once all policies are validated and the firewall has been observed under real conditions, it can be placed into production, and continuous monitoring should begin to ensure the firewall performs as intended and adapts to any changes in the network environment.

Chapter 4: Defining Security Zones and Policies

Defining security zones and policies is a foundational step in building an effective firewall strategy, as it allows administrators to group network assets based on trust levels, function, or risk, and to apply access control policies that reflect the organization's security posture. A **security zone** is a logical or physical segment of the network where all connected systems share the same level of trust and security requirements. These zones are typically defined by assigning firewall interfaces to specific roles, such as internal, external, DMZ, guest, or management. Each zone represents a distinct environment, and the firewall enforces rules that govern the traffic flowing between them. This approach enables clear boundaries and makes it easier to apply consistent and meaningful policies across the network.

The most common security zones include the **internal zone**, which contains trusted systems such as workstations, servers, and internal applications; the **external zone**, which represents untrusted networks such as the internet; and the **DMZ**, which is a semi-trusted zone used to host publicly accessible services like web servers, email gateways, or DNS servers. By placing public-facing services in the DMZ rather than the internal network, administrators reduce the risk that a compromise of those systems will lead to deeper intrusion. In more advanced architectures, additional zones might be created for wireless networks, partner networks, development environments, or critical infrastructure systems, each with its own security requirements and access restrictions.

Once the zones are defined, the next step is to create **policies**, which are sets of rules that specify which types of traffic are allowed or denied between zones. These policies are based on multiple criteria, including source and destination IP addresses, ports, protocols, users, applications, and even time of day. Firewalls evaluate these policies in a specific order, and the first rule that matches the traffic determines the outcome. For this reason, the order and specificity of rules are critical. Broad rules placed too high in the policy chain can override more restrictive rules below them, potentially creating unintended access paths or security holes.

Best practices recommend starting with a **default deny policy**, meaning all traffic between zones is blocked unless explicitly permitted by a rule. This approach supports the principle of least privilege, where access is granted only when necessary for business purposes. Once this baseline is established, individual rules can be created to allow specific types of traffic, such as HTTP from internal users to the internet, or database access between application servers and backend systems. It is also important to consider directionality; policies can be configured to allow traffic only in one direction, which helps prevent lateral movement by attackers in the event of a compromise.

As firewalls become more sophisticated, policies are no longer limited to IP addresses and ports. **Next-generation firewalls** support identity-based policies that enforce rules based on user or group membership, as well as application-level policies that recognize and control specific types of applications regardless of port or protocol. This allows for more granular control, such as permitting only members of the finance department to access payroll applications or blocking unauthorized file-sharing software while allowing web browsing. These contextual controls increase the effectiveness of firewall policies and better align with how users interact with systems and data.

Policy documentation and organization are critical for long-term maintainability. Each rule should have a clear name, description, and justification, making it easier for administrators to review and audit the rules over time. Unused or duplicate rules should be regularly identified and removed to reduce complexity and prevent misconfigurations. Policy review processes should be formalized and conducted periodically to ensure that firewall rules continue to reflect current network structures, business requirements, and security threats. Change control procedures must also be followed when modifying policies, especially in large or regulated environments, to prevent accidental service disruption or the introduction of vulnerabilities.

In segmented networks, defining policies between zones allows for **microsegmentation**, where access between individual systems or applications is tightly controlled. This is especially important in environments with high security requirements, such as data centers, healthcare, or financial services, where a single point of entry must not provide attackers with access to the entire network. By carefully defining security zones and aligning firewall policies to enforce appropriate boundaries, organizations gain better visibility, tighter control, and stronger protection against internal and external threats.

Chapter 5: Writing Effective Firewall Rules

Writing effective firewall rules is one of the most important tasks in securing a network, as these rules determine which types of traffic are permitted or denied across various parts of the infrastructure. A firewall rule is composed of several parameters that define the conditions under which a packet or session is allowed to proceed or must be blocked. These parameters typically include source and destination IP addresses, ports, protocols, traffic direction, action (allow or deny), and sometimes user identity or application context in the case of next-generation firewalls. Crafting these rules requires a clear understanding of the network architecture, the services in use, the roles of users and devices, and the potential threats that must be mitigated.

The first step in writing effective firewall rules is to base them on a well-defined security policy. This policy should outline what is considered acceptable and necessary traffic, based on business requirements, operational needs, and regulatory constraints. From this policy, administrators can derive specific rules that reflect the principle of least privilege, where only traffic that is essential for legitimate communication is allowed. By default, all other traffic should be denied. This approach ensures that the firewall enforces intentional and controlled access rather than leaving security to assumptions or undefined behavior.

Firewall rules should be as specific as possible to reduce ambiguity and limit the risk of unintended access. For example, instead of allowing all traffic from a network segment to the internet, a rule might allow only HTTPS traffic (TCP port 443) from the internal network to specific external destinations. When rules are too broad or vague, they can create security gaps that are difficult to detect and even harder to audit. Granular rules make it easier to pinpoint unusual activity and apply targeted changes without disrupting legitimate services. At the same time, care must be taken to avoid creating an overly complex rule base, which can lead to performance issues and administrative errors.

Another best practice in writing firewall rules is to group related objects using address groups, port groups, or service objects. These groupings help simplify rule sets and improve readability. For instance, rather than creating separate rules for each server in the accounting department, an administrator can create an address group named "Accounting_Servers" and apply a single rule that applies to the group as a whole. This approach not only reduces the number of rules but also makes maintenance more manageable as changes can be made to the object definitions without needing to edit every individual rule.

Ordering rules correctly is critical, as firewalls typically evaluate rules from top to bottom and apply the first match encountered. A more general rule placed above a more specific one may inadvertently allow or deny traffic that should have been handled differently. Therefore, specific allow or deny rules should be placed above more general rules to ensure proper enforcement. Periodic rule reviews and cleanups are essential to remove obsolete entries, eliminate redundancy, and maintain clarity in the rule base. Tools that provide hit counters or rule usage statistics can help identify unused or ineffective rules that can safely be removed or consolidated.

Comments and documentation should accompany every rule to explain its purpose, origin, and the person or team responsible for requesting it. This practice improves transparency, accountability, and the ability to troubleshoot issues when they arise. Well-documented rules also help during audits and when handing over firewall responsibilities to new administrators. In large environments, firewalls should also support role-based access control, so that only authorized personnel can edit rules and changes are logged for accountability.

With the increasing use of dynamic services and cloud-based infrastructure, firewalls that support dynamic or adaptive rulesets can be highly valuable. These firewalls can automatically adjust rules based on real-time context such as device posture, user authentication status, or threat intelligence feeds. For example, if a specific IP is flagged as malicious by a threat feed, the firewall can automatically block traffic to or from that address without requiring manual intervention. Writing firewall rules that incorporate such dynamic elements adds a layer of agility to the security posture, enabling faster responses to emerging threats.

Firewall rules should be tested in a controlled environment when possible before being deployed in production. Simulation tools or nonintrusive monitoring can be used to observe the potential impact of new rules and ensure that they do not unintentionally block critical traffic. Continuous monitoring and logging help confirm that rules are functioning as intended and allow administrators to detect any anomalies or misconfigurations. Writing effective firewall rules is an ongoing process that requires both strategic planning and detailed technical execution, combining clarity, precision, and adaptability to maintain strong, responsive network security.

Chapter 6: Managing Rule Order and Rule Optimization

Managing rule order and rule optimization is a critical aspect of firewall administration that directly impacts both security effectiveness and network performance. Firewalls evaluate rules in a sequential manner, usually from top to bottom, stopping at the first rule that matches the traffic criteria. This means that the order in which rules are written and arranged can determine how traffic is handled, even if multiple rules could potentially apply. Misordered rules may allow traffic that should be blocked, block traffic that should be allowed, or cause unnecessary processing overhead as the firewall evaluates too many irrelevant rules before finding a match. Understanding how rule order influences behavior is essential for building a clean, efficient, and secure rule base.

The process of rule evaluation begins with a packet or session entering the firewall and being compared against the list of rules. If the first rule matches the source and destination IP addresses, ports, and protocols, the firewall applies the corresponding action—allow or deny—and stops further evaluation. If no match is found, the firewall continues down the rule list until it either finds a match or reaches the end, where an implicit deny rule typically blocks all unmatched traffic. This behavior highlights the importance of placing specific rules above general ones. For example, a rule that allows internal DNS servers to communicate with external root servers on UDP port 53 should come before a general rule that blocks all outbound UDP traffic. If the general rule appears first, the specific DNS rule may never be evaluated, and legitimate DNS queries could be blocked.

Rule optimization begins with identifying redundant, overlapping, or conflicting rules that may complicate the firewall's behavior or reduce its performance. Over time, as administrators make changes to firewall policies—whether to accommodate new services, respond to incidents, or address user requests—the rule base can become bloated with entries that no longer serve a purpose or were added without considering existing rules. This clutter increases the processing time required to evaluate each packet and can make it difficult to maintain or troubleshoot the firewall configuration. Regular audits should be performed to review the rule set, verify each rule's purpose, and remove or consolidate any unnecessary entries.

Firewall platforms often provide **hit counters**, which track how many times each rule has been matched. These counters can help identify rules that are never triggered, suggesting they may be obsolete or incorrectly configured. Administrators should use this data, along with traffic logs, to refine the rule order. Frequently used rules—especially those that match high volumes of legitimate traffic—should be placed closer to the top of the rule list to reduce the amount of processing required for common scenarios. This practice can improve throughput and reduce latency, especially in firewalls handling large amounts of traffic.

Another aspect of optimization involves the use of **rule grouping and object reuse**. Instead of writing separate rules for every individual IP address or service, administrators can create address groups, service objects, or application groups. This not only simplifies the rule base but also makes it easier to apply changes consistently across multiple policies. For example, if a new server is added to the HR subnet, it can simply be included in the existing "HR_Network" object rather than requiring the creation of multiple new rules.

Conflicting rules are another common issue in poorly optimized rule sets. A rule that allows traffic may be inadvertently overridden by a broader deny rule placed higher in the list, or vice versa. Detecting and resolving these conflicts requires a clear understanding of the intended access controls and careful analysis of how rules interact. In some cases, rule simulation tools or policy analyzers provided by firewall vendors can assist in identifying inconsistencies, shadows, or anomalies in the rule set.

Proper documentation is essential for rule management and optimization. Each rule should include metadata such as a clear name, description, creation date, last modification date, and the identity of the person who added it. This information supports accountability, simplifies audits, and helps new team members understand the logic behind the rule base. When managing rule order and optimization across multiple firewalls or sites, centralized management platforms can provide a unified interface for rule editing, synchronization, and compliance enforcement. These platforms often include built-in optimization tools that suggest rule reordering or highlight inefficiencies. Rule management is not a one-time task but an ongoing process that must adapt to changes in network architecture, business requirements, and the evolving threat landscape. Efficient rule sets enable faster processing, easier maintenance, and more predictable firewall behavior, all of which contribute to stronger and more resilient network security.

Chapter 7: Handling Inbound and Outbound Traffic

Handling inbound and outbound traffic is one of the primary responsibilities of a firewall, and it requires a clear understanding of traffic direction, trust boundaries, and the types of services and connections used within the network. Inbound traffic refers to data packets originating from outside the network—typically from the internet or another external network—and destined for internal hosts or services. Outbound traffic, by contrast, originates from within the internal network and is directed toward external destinations. Firewalls must be configured to inspect, filter, and control both types of traffic based on security policies that align with business needs, user roles, and risk management strategies.

When managing **inbound traffic**, the primary concern is preventing unauthorized access to internal systems while still allowing legitimate requests to reach public-facing services. Most organizations host certain services—such as websites, email servers, or remote access portals—that need to be accessible from the outside. To safely allow this, firewalls are typically configured with **destination NAT (DNAT)** or **port forwarding** rules, which redirect incoming requests on specific public IP addresses and ports to corresponding internal servers. These rules must be tightly controlled and limited only to the ports and protocols required for the service to function. For example, if a web server must be accessible to the public, only TCP ports 80 and 443 should be opened, and all other ports should remain blocked. Access to administrative interfaces or sensitive services should never be exposed directly to the internet unless secured through VPNs or authentication gateways.

To further reduce the attack surface for inbound traffic, services exposed to the internet should be placed in a **demilitarized zone (DMZ)**—a separate network segment designed to isolate externally accessible systems from the trusted internal network. The firewall acts as a gatekeeper between the DMZ and both the internal and external zones, enforcing strict rules to limit traffic flow. For example, a web server in the DMZ might be allowed to initiate database queries to a backend server in the internal network on a specific port, but all other connections from the DMZ to the internal network would be denied. This segmentation ensures that even if a publicly accessible service is compromised, the attacker's ability to move laterally into the core network is limited.

Outbound traffic, while often considered less risky, also requires careful scrutiny. Many organizations allow internal users or systems to initiate outbound connections without restrictions, which can lead to significant security issues. Malicious software installed on an internal host may use outbound connections to communicate with command-and-control servers, exfiltrate sensitive data, or download additional payloads. To mitigate this, firewalls should be configured with **egress filtering**, which involves setting rules that control what types of outbound traffic are permitted, from which sources, to which destinations, and on which ports and protocols. For example, an organization might allow only HTTP, HTTPS, and DNS traffic from user workstations, while blocking all outbound traffic from servers that should not initiate external connections.

A key component of handling both inbound and outbound traffic is **deep packet inspection (DPI)**, which allows firewalls to analyze the contents of data packets beyond just the header information.

This enables the detection of malicious payloads, protocol anomalies, or application misuse within permitted traffic flows. DPI is especially valuable in outbound traffic monitoring, as it can detect data leakage, botnet activity, or attempts to tunnel unauthorized protocols through allowed ports. Firewalls that support application-aware filtering can also identify specific applications within generic traffic and apply more granular controls, such as allowing access to Microsoft Teams while blocking other file-sharing tools over the same ports.

Logging and monitoring of both inbound and outbound traffic is essential for visibility and incident response. Administrators should review logs to identify abnormal patterns, such as repeated failed login attempts on inbound SSH connections or large volumes of outbound data transfers from a single host. These logs can also help refine firewall rules over time, by identifying unnecessary traffic, misconfigured services, or emerging threats. Integrating the firewall with a Security Information and Event Management (SIEM) system enables correlation of traffic events with other security data, improving the ability to detect and respond to attacks that span multiple stages.

Balancing security and functionality in firewall rules for inbound and outbound traffic is a dynamic process that requires constant evaluation. New services, business applications, and user behaviors can all affect the nature of network traffic and may necessitate updates to firewall policies. Regular rule reviews, traffic analysis, and testing are necessary to ensure that the firewall continues to enforce the organization's security goals while enabling legitimate communication across network boundaries.

Chapter 8: Configuring NAT, VPNs, and Remote Access

Configuring NAT, VPNs, and remote access on a firewall involves a combination of network translation, secure tunneling, and controlled user entry into internal systems, all of which are essential for modern network functionality and security. **Network Address Translation (NAT)** is typically the first of these components to be configured, as it allows private IP addresses within an internal network to communicate with external systems using public IPs. NAT is often required due to the limited availability of IPv4 addresses and the need to mask internal network structures from the outside world. Firewalls perform NAT by modifying the IP headers of packets, replacing private source addresses with public addresses for outbound traffic and mapping incoming responses back to the original internal devices. Static NAT may be used when a consistent one-to-one mapping is needed, such as for hosting a public-facing server, while dynamic NAT or Port Address Translation (PAT) allows multiple internal devices to share a single public IP address through the use of unique port assignments.

The configuration of NAT rules must be carefully planned to avoid IP conflicts, ensure that the correct internal systems are reachable, and prevent exposing unnecessary services to the internet. For instance, port forwarding—a feature of NAT used to direct specific traffic from the public interface to an internal device—must be limited to only required services, such as HTTP, HTTPS, or SSH, and further restricted to known IP sources whenever possible. Firewall policies should work in tandem with NAT rules to define which traffic is allowed through the translation layer, adding another level of control and inspection.

In addition to NAT, configuring **Virtual Private Networks (VPNs)** on the firewall is crucial for secure communication between remote users or branch offices and the main network. VPNs use encryption and tunneling protocols to create secure pathways over untrusted networks, such as the internet, allowing data to travel safely between endpoints. There are two main types of VPNs managed through a firewall: **site-to-site VPNs** and **remote access VPNs**. Site-to-site VPNs connect entire networks to each other, such as linking a corporate headquarters with regional branches. These tunnels are typically established using IPsec (Internet Protocol Security), a suite of protocols that provides confidentiality, integrity, and authentication. Configuration involves defining tunnel endpoints, shared keys or certificates, encryption algorithms, and routing rules to ensure that traffic destined for the remote network is sent through the VPN.

Remote access VPNs, on the other hand, are designed for individual users who need to connect to the internal network from home, hotels, or other offsite locations. These VPNs often use SSL or IPsec and can be configured with client software or browser-based portals. Firewalls that support remote access VPNs must be configured to authenticate users using credentials, multi-factor authentication (MFA), or certificates. Access control policies should define which internal systems users can reach once connected, based on their roles or group memberships. Logging and monitoring are essential for auditing user activity and identifying suspicious behavior within remote sessions.

Configuring VPNs also involves ensuring **high availability and failover**, especially for site-to-site connections, where loss of connectivity can disrupt business operations. Redundant tunnels and dynamic routing protocols such as BGP or OSPF may be used to maintain connectivity even if one path becomes unavailable. VPN performance should also be considered, as encryption and decryption require processing resources. Firewalls must be capable of handling the expected number of simultaneous VPN sessions without degradation in throughput or latency.

The third key area—**remote access configuration**—extends beyond VPNs and may include direct access to web applications, virtual desktops, or cloud-based services. Firewalls can be configured as application gateways or reverse proxies, enabling secure access to specific internal services without requiring full network-level connectivity. Remote access portals often include web-based interfaces secured with SSL/TLS and can integrate with authentication systems such as LDAP, RADIUS, or cloud-based identity providers. Role-based access controls and session timeouts enhance security by ensuring that users access only what they need for the duration of their session. In environments with bring-your-own-device (BYOD) policies, firewalls may also perform endpoint posture checks before allowing access, verifying factors like antivirus status, operating system updates, or device certificates.

Effective configuration of NAT, VPNs, and remote access ensures that internal resources are protected, connectivity is maintained across distributed environments, and remote workers can perform their duties securely and efficiently. All these components must be continuously monitored and updated to reflect changes in infrastructure, user roles, and the evolving threat landscape.

Chapter 9: High Availability and Failover Setup

High availability and failover setup are essential components in enterprise firewall deployments where continuous network access, service uptime, and security enforcement are critical. A single firewall operating as the sole point of inspection creates a potential single point of failure; if that device fails due to hardware malfunction, software error, or power loss, the entire network's connectivity and protection could be disrupted. To avoid such outages and maintain uninterrupted service, organizations deploy firewalls in **high availability (HA)** configurations, which involve multiple firewall units working together to ensure continuity of service even during failure scenarios. These configurations typically include a **primary** or **active** firewall and a **secondary** or **standby** firewall that takes over in case the primary becomes unavailable.

The two most common HA models are **active/passive** and **active/active**. In an **active/passive** configuration, one firewall handles all traffic while the other remains idle, continuously monitoring the health of the active unit. If the active firewall fails, the passive unit detects the failure through a heartbeat mechanism and takes over the role of traffic processing with minimal disruption. This switchover, often called a **failover**, must happen quickly to maintain application and network availability, and the transition should be seamless to end users. In contrast, **active/active** configurations have both firewalls handling traffic simultaneously, often with load balancing to distribute the processing load between them. This setup not only provides redundancy but also improves performance and throughput, although it requires more complex configuration and synchronization between the two units.

Regardless of the chosen model, the firewalls in an HA pair must remain synchronized to avoid inconsistencies that could lead to service interruptions during failover. Synchronization includes maintaining identical firewall rules, NAT policies, session tables, configurations, and licensing. In stateful failover scenarios, even active session information is shared between the devices so that ongoing connections do not need to be re-established when failover occurs. This is particularly important for applications like VoIP calls, VPN tunnels, or database sessions, where reinitializing a session could lead to dropped connections, data loss, or degraded user experience. Synchronization is usually managed through a dedicated **HA link**, which allows the firewalls to exchange state and configuration data in real time.

Setting up high availability also involves ensuring **redundant network paths,** which means connecting both firewalls to the same upstream and downstream switches or routers using separate physical interfaces. Redundant cabling, power supplies, and network paths are necessary to eliminate single points of failure in the surrounding infrastructure. In more advanced environments, firewalls may be placed in separate data centers or physical locations and connected through high-speed links to provide geographic redundancy. Such configurations help maintain availability even in the case of localized disasters or power outages.

Firewalls in HA mode should also be monitored and tested regularly to confirm that failover mechanisms are functioning correctly. Periodic **failover testing** involves simulating failures—such as disconnecting a power source, disabling a network interface, or triggering a crash—to verify that the secondary firewall correctly assumes control without impacting connectivity. Logs and alerts generated during these tests should be reviewed to ensure that switchover is smooth and within acceptable time thresholds. Monitoring tools should be integrated with the organization's network operations center or security information and event management (SIEM) platform to provide real-time visibility into the health and status of the HA pair.

Another consideration in high availability is the **licensing and feature parity** between the two firewall units. In many commercial firewall solutions, both units must have identical licenses for features such as VPN, intrusion prevention, or antivirus filtering to function correctly during failover. Mismatched capabilities can lead to unexpected behavior, such as loss of features or blocked traffic when the secondary unit takes over. As part of the initial setup and ongoing maintenance, administrators must ensure that all software versions, firmware updates, and licenses are kept in sync across both units.

High availability and failover strategies must also account for **maintenance and upgrade scenarios**, where planned downtime of one firewall should not affect the availability of services. With a properly configured HA setup, firmware updates or configuration changes can be applied to one unit at a time, allowing traffic to continue flowing through the other without disruption. This approach ensures business continuity, minimizes maintenance windows, and supports compliance with uptime requirements often specified in service-level agreements. Through careful planning, configuration, and testing, HA and failover ensure that firewall services remain resilient and that network security remains enforceable under all conditions.

Chapter 10: Backup, Maintenance, and Disaster Recovery Planning

Backup, maintenance, and disaster recovery planning are essential components of managing a firewall infrastructure, ensuring that security configurations are preserved, systems remain operational, and recovery is possible in the event of failures or catastrophic events. A firewall, being a critical point of control and protection for any network, must be maintained with the same rigor as any core IT system. Configuration changes, rule updates, firmware upgrades, and integration with other services are part of its ongoing life cycle, and each of these changes introduces a potential point of failure if not handled properly. To mitigate these risks, administrators must implement a structured process for creating backups of firewall configurations, documenting change history, and developing a clear disaster recovery plan that can be executed under pressure.

The first layer of preparedness involves **regular configuration backups**, which capture the current state of the firewall's settings, including access control lists, NAT rules, VPN configurations, logging preferences, firmware versions, and user accounts. These backups should be scheduled automatically and stored securely on a system that is separate from the firewall itself. Many firewall platforms support encrypted backups and can integrate with centralized storage or backup servers. A best practice is to retain multiple versions of the backup files, allowing for rollback to a known good state in case a recent change introduces problems. The naming convention of backup files, timestamps, and change logs should be organized to quickly identify the backup associated with a particular configuration state or incident.

In addition to backing up configurations, firewalls should be included in broader **maintenance schedules**, just like switches, routers, and servers. Maintenance activities include applying firmware and software updates, reviewing rule sets for redundancy or inefficiencies, validating license statuses, and checking system health indicators such as CPU usage, memory utilization, and interface performance. Firmware updates often include critical security patches or new features that improve firewall capabilities, and delaying these updates can leave systems exposed to vulnerabilities. Before any update is applied, backups must be created to ensure that the device can be restored to a functioning state in case the update fails or causes unexpected issues. Maintenance windows should be carefully planned during off-peak hours, with change management procedures in place to document the rationale for the update, the expected impact, and the rollback steps if problems occur.

Disaster recovery planning begins with identifying the potential failure scenarios that could impact the firewall infrastructure. These include hardware failures, software corruption, configuration errors, natural disasters, or cyberattacks that render the firewall inoperable. The recovery plan should outline the steps required to restore firewall functionality, including how to provision new hardware or virtual appliances, how to load the most recent configuration backup, and how to verify that restored systems are functioning correctly. For firewalls deployed in high-availability pairs, the plan must include steps for replacing a failed node and reintegrating it into the HA cluster without disrupting traffic. In cloud or hybrid environments, where virtual firewalls may be spun up in minutes, recovery plans must also cover orchestration scripts, access credentials, and integration with network segments and security groups.

Communication during a disaster recovery scenario is just as important as the technical response. The plan should designate roles and responsibilities for the recovery team, include contact information for key personnel and vendors, and specify how stakeholders will be informed of progress and resolution. Testing the disaster recovery plan through tabletop exercises or simulated failovers helps ensure that the plan is realistic, comprehensive, and executable under real-world stress. These tests also reveal weaknesses in documentation, gaps in the backup process, or dependencies that were not previously identified.

Firewall logs and audit trails are also part of the recovery ecosystem. Reviewing logs after an incident helps determine the cause of failure and whether it was due to misconfiguration, unauthorized access, or hardware degradation. These insights can guide future preventive measures, such as improved monitoring, more restrictive change policies, or hardware upgrades. Finally, every recovery should be followed by a post-incident review to assess what worked, what didn't, and how the organization can better prepare for the next event. Integrating firewalls into a broader disaster recovery and business continuity strategy ensures that network security can be restored quickly and reliably, preserving trust, compliance, and operational integrity in the face of disruption.

BOOK 3
ADVANCED THREAT DETECTION AND RESPONSE: INTEGRATING FIREWALLS WITH MODERN SECURITY SYSTEMS

ROB BOTWRIGHT

Chapter 1: The Changing Threat Landscape

The changing threat landscape is a defining factor in how modern network security strategies are developed and deployed, and it has evolved dramatically over the past two decades. What once consisted primarily of amateur hackers seeking notoriety has transformed into a complex ecosystem of advanced persistent threats, financially motivated cybercriminals, hacktivist groups, and state-sponsored actors, all leveraging increasingly sophisticated tools and tactics. The traditional model of defending a static network perimeter has become less effective as threats now often originate from within, move laterally across internal systems, and target not only infrastructure but also applications, identities, and data. Firewalls, intrusion prevention systems, endpoint protection, and access control mechanisms must all be adapted to confront these emerging threats.

One of the most significant changes in the threat landscape is the rise of **ransomware**, which has shifted from isolated, opportunistic attacks to highly organized operations that target specific organizations, often after a period of reconnaissance. Attackers gain initial access through phishing emails, exposed remote desktop services, or compromised credentials, and then move stealthily through the network to identify critical assets before deploying the ransomware payload. Modern ransomware operators not only encrypt data but also exfiltrate sensitive information to increase leverage through extortion, threatening to publish stolen data unless a ransom is paid. This double-extortion tactic has increased the pressure on organizations and highlighted the need for layered defenses and rapid detection and response capabilities.

Another major evolution in threats is the widespread use of **living-off-the-land techniques**, where attackers use legitimate tools and services already present in the environment to avoid detection. Tools like PowerShell, Windows Management Instrumentation (WMI), and remote administration utilities are frequently abused to conduct reconnaissance, escalate privileges, move laterally, and maintain persistence without triggering traditional antivirus or firewall alerts. These attacks blend into normal activity and require behavioral analytics and anomaly detection to uncover, shifting the focus from simple signature-based detection to a more nuanced understanding of how systems and users typically behave.

The growing dependence on cloud services and remote access has introduced new attack surfaces and complexities. **Misconfigured cloud resources**, weak identity management practices, and a lack of visibility into east-west traffic in cloud environments have enabled attackers to bypass traditional perimeter defenses. Attackers may exploit vulnerabilities in cloud-hosted applications or abuse exposed APIs to gain unauthorized access. In many cases, organizations are unaware of their full exposure due to shadow IT or inadequate cloud security posture management. As a result, modern security strategies must extend to cloud-native firewalls, identity-based access controls, and continuous monitoring of workloads across hybrid and multi-cloud environments.

Supply chain attacks have also emerged as a serious threat, where attackers compromise a third-party vendor or software provider to reach their intended targets. The SolarWinds and Kaseya breaches demonstrated how attackers can use trusted software update mechanisms to distribute malware to thousands of organizations simultaneously. This type of threat is especially difficult to defend against because it exploits trust relationships rather than technical vulnerabilities. Organizations must now evaluate the security posture of their vendors and partners and implement controls to detect anomalous behavior even in systems that are assumed to be safe.

Social engineering and phishing remain among the most common initial access vectors, but the sophistication of these attacks has increased. Phishing emails now often use carefully crafted messages that mimic legitimate communications, sometimes personalized using publicly available information to increase their credibility. Spear phishing and business email compromise (BEC) attacks can trick employees into transferring funds or disclosing sensitive credentials. These attacks bypass technical defenses and exploit human behavior, necessitating a combination of user awareness training, email filtering, and real-time threat detection to mitigate risk.

Attackers are increasingly using **automation, artificial intelligence, and machine learning** to scale their operations and improve evasion. Malicious bots scan the internet for vulnerable systems, launch brute-force attacks, and test stolen credentials across multiple services. Malware now often includes polymorphic code that changes its appearance with each infection, making it harder to detect using traditional antivirus tools. This has driven the need for adaptive defense mechanisms that can analyze patterns, correlate signals across multiple systems, and respond in real-time.

As the threat landscape continues to change, organizations must shift from a reactive mindset to a proactive one, employing continuous risk assessments, real-time monitoring, and a zero trust approach to security. This evolving environment demands not only technical controls but also cultural changes in how cybersecurity is approached, managed, and embedded into the operational fabric of every organization.

Chapter 2: Deep Packet Inspection and Application Awareness

Deep packet inspection and application awareness are critical capabilities in modern firewalls, enabling far more sophisticated control over network traffic than traditional filtering methods based solely on ports, protocols, and IP addresses. Deep packet inspection, commonly abbreviated as DPI, refers to the process of examining not just the header of a data packet but also its payload—the actual content being transmitted. This allows the firewall to analyze traffic at a much deeper level and make decisions based on the nature of the data itself, rather than only on where it's coming from or what port it's using. DPI enables the identification of specific applications, detection of anomalies, enforcement of compliance policies, and the blocking of malicious content even when it attempts to disguise itself within legitimate-looking traffic.

Traditional firewalls operated at layers 3 and 4 of the OSI model, primarily focusing on IP addresses and TCP or UDP port numbers to allow or deny traffic. While effective in earlier network environments, this approach has become inadequate as modern applications frequently use dynamic ports, encrypted connections, and sophisticated evasion techniques to bypass security controls. For example, a peer-to-peer file sharing application might use the same port as HTTPS traffic, making it indistinguishable to a traditional port-based firewall. Deep packet inspection, however, allows the firewall to look beyond the port number and identify the application based on its signature, behavior, or even specific data patterns contained within the payload.

Application awareness goes hand-in-hand with DPI and refers to the firewall's ability to recognize, classify, and control traffic based on the specific application generating it. Instead of treating all traffic on port 443 as equal, for example, an application-aware firewall can distinguish between Microsoft Teams, Zoom, Dropbox, or a web browser session using that same port. This level of visibility allows organizations to enforce highly granular security policies that align more closely with business requirements. For instance, a company may allow the use of Office 365 while blocking unauthorized file-sharing applications, even though both types of traffic may appear identical from a port and protocol perspective.

The ability to identify applications accurately also enables better bandwidth management and quality of service (QoS) enforcement. By recognizing which applications are consuming bandwidth, firewalls can prioritize critical business applications while throttling or restricting less important or potentially risky traffic. This is especially useful in environments with limited network capacity or where performance of specific services must be guaranteed. Additionally, application-aware firewalls can log detailed information about application usage, helping administrators monitor user behavior, detect policy violations, and conduct forensic analysis after a security incident.

Another key benefit of DPI and application awareness is their role in detecting and preventing evasive threats. Modern malware often uses encryption, tunneling, or even hijacking of legitimate protocols to bypass conventional security measures. DPI can analyze traffic for indicators of compromise, such as command-and-control communications hidden within otherwise benign sessions, or embedded malicious code in files transferred through email or web services. Coupled with application identification, this allows firewalls to apply advanced threat protection techniques, including sandboxing, protocol validation, and behavior-based detection, to prevent exploitation and data exfiltration.

However, implementing deep packet inspection does require significant processing power and memory, especially in high-throughput environments or when dealing with encrypted traffic. As a result, DPI features are typically found in next-generation firewalls (NGFWs) that are designed with specialized hardware and optimized software to handle the additional inspection workload. When inspecting encrypted traffic, the firewall must perform SSL/TLS decryption and then re-encrypt the traffic after inspection, a process that must be done securely and in compliance with privacy policies and regulatory requirements.

The visibility gained through DPI and application awareness also supports compliance and audit efforts. Many regulatory standards require organizations to control and monitor data flows to ensure sensitive information is protected. By identifying applications and inspecting data payloads, firewalls can enforce policies that restrict the use of unapproved services or block the transmission of specific data types, such as credit card numbers or personally identifiable information. Application-aware controls can also be used to enforce acceptable use policies, blocking access to gaming, streaming, or social media services during work hours while allowing access to business-critical resources.

Deep packet inspection and application awareness transform firewalls from basic gatekeepers into intelligent, context-aware security platforms that understand not just where traffic is going, but what it is and why it matters. This level of understanding is essential for effective policy enforcement, threat detection, bandwidth control, and overall network visibility in today's complex, encrypted, and application-driven environments.

Chapter 3: Intrusion Detection and Prevention Systems (IDS/IPS)

Intrusion Detection and Prevention Systems, commonly referred to as IDS and IPS, are critical components of a modern cybersecurity architecture, especially when integrated with or placed alongside firewalls. Both IDS and IPS are designed to monitor network traffic for signs of malicious activity, policy violations, or abnormal behavior, but they serve slightly different roles. An **Intrusion Detection System (IDS)** is a monitoring tool that analyzes network or system traffic and generates alerts when it detects suspicious patterns that may indicate a threat or attack. It is passive in nature, meaning it does not take action to block the traffic but instead notifies administrators or security systems for further investigation. By contrast, an **Intrusion Prevention System (IPS)** takes a more active approach. It not only detects potential threats but also takes immediate action to block or mitigate them, such as dropping malicious packets, resetting connections, or reconfiguring firewall rules dynamically to prevent further exploitation.

The primary function of both IDS and IPS technologies is to identify attack signatures and anomalies. Signature-based detection relies on a database of known attack patterns, such as specific byte sequences or behaviors associated with malware, exploits, or unauthorized access attempts. These signatures are regularly updated by vendors to keep pace with evolving threats. While this method is effective for recognizing known attacks, it may struggle to detect zero-day exploits or new variants of malware that have not yet been documented. To address this limitation, many IDS and IPS systems also incorporate **anomaly-based detection**, which involves establishing a baseline of normal network behavior and then identifying deviations that could indicate malicious activity. This allows for the detection of previously unknown threats, although it may result in higher false positive rates if not properly tuned.

Placement of IDS and IPS sensors within the network is crucial to their effectiveness. An IDS is typically deployed in a **promiscuous mode**, meaning it receives a copy of traffic via a network tap or a span port and analyzes it without interfering with the flow of traffic. This is useful for environments where high availability is critical, and where the organization prefers to avoid introducing latency. An IPS, on the other hand, is usually deployed **inline**, meaning all traffic passes through it and can be actively filtered or blocked if necessary. Inline deployment ensures immediate threat mitigation but requires careful configuration and resource allocation to avoid becoming a bottleneck or point of failure.

Modern IDS/IPS solutions are often integrated into **next-generation firewalls (NGFWs)**, creating a unified threat management platform that combines packet inspection, signature matching, application awareness, and real-time threat response. This integration enhances visibility and streamlines management, allowing security teams to enforce policies based not only on IP addresses and ports but also on user identities, applications, and detected threats. When a threat is identified, the IPS component can automatically quarantine affected systems, block attacker IPs, or trigger alerts in a centralized security information and event management (SIEM) system. These automated responses significantly reduce the time between detection and mitigation, improving the organization's ability to contain threats before they cause damage.

One of the key challenges in operating IDS and IPS systems is minimizing **false positives and false negatives**. A false positive occurs when benign traffic is incorrectly identified as malicious, leading to unnecessary alerts or blocked services. Too many false positives can overwhelm security teams and reduce confidence in the alerts being generated. A false negative, on the other hand, occurs when actual malicious activity goes undetected, leaving the network vulnerable to attack. To maintain accuracy, IDS/IPS systems must be regularly updated, fine-tuned, and configured in alignment with the network's unique traffic patterns and business needs.

Another important aspect of IDS/IPS functionality is **deep packet inspection (DPI),** which allows the system to analyze the payload of packets rather than just the headers. This is particularly useful in identifying application-layer attacks, such as SQL injection, cross-site scripting, or buffer overflow attempts, that may not be detectable through basic packet filtering. DPI also enables content-based filtering and data loss prevention by scanning for sensitive information such as credit card numbers or personally identifiable information being transmitted without authorization.

To ensure the effectiveness of IDS and IPS, organizations must also implement **log analysis, threat intelligence integration, and regular testing**. Logs generated by these systems should be collected, correlated, and analyzed to identify trends, understand attacker behavior, and improve detection rules. Threat intelligence feeds can enhance detection capabilities by providing up-to-date information on known malicious IPs, domains, and attack vectors. Periodic penetration testing and red team exercises can help validate the efficacy of IDS/IPS systems and uncover any weaknesses in detection or response workflows. Through consistent maintenance, strategic placement, and intelligent integration, IDS and IPS technologies play a vital role in modern network defense, helping to detect, disrupt, and prevent a wide range of cyber threats.

Chapter 4: Integrating Firewalls with SIEM Platforms

Integrating firewalls with SIEM (Security Information and Event Management) platforms is a vital step in building a centralized, intelligent, and responsive cybersecurity architecture. Firewalls generate a vast amount of valuable data, including traffic logs, rule matches, denied connection attempts, protocol usage, and intrusion alerts, but on their own, these logs often remain underutilized. Without centralized collection, correlation, and analysis, critical security events may be missed, alerts may go unnoticed, and the organization may lack the broader context necessary to detect advanced threats. A SIEM platform addresses these challenges by aggregating logs from multiple sources, normalizing the data, applying correlation rules, and providing security analysts with real-time alerts, dashboards, and forensic tools.

The first step in integration involves configuring the firewall to send log data to the SIEM platform. This is typically done using standard protocols such as **Syslog**, **SNMP traps**, or **API-based connectors**, depending on the firewall vendor and SIEM capabilities. Administrators must determine which types of logs to forward, including traffic logs, threat logs, authentication logs, and system events.

Care must be taken not to overload the SIEM with excessive or irrelevant data, so log filtering and prioritization are essential. For example, high-value events such as denied connections to sensitive ports, repeated failed login attempts, or triggers from intrusion prevention systems should be forwarded in real time, while routine allow logs can be aggregated or sampled based on volume and necessity.

Once logs are being collected by the SIEM, the next step is **log normalization**, where data from different firewall models and formats is transformed into a standardized schema that the SIEM can interpret. This enables correlation across different sources, such as combining firewall events with data from endpoints, servers, authentication systems, and threat intelligence feeds. For instance, a login attempt from an unusual IP address that also corresponds to a spike in denied firewall traffic to admin interfaces can be flagged as a high-priority event when analyzed in context. This ability to connect disparate events into a coherent narrative is one of the core advantages of SIEM integration and plays a key role in detecting complex attacks like lateral movement, privilege escalation, and data exfiltration.

SIEM platforms also enhance visibility through **dashboards and visualizations**, allowing security teams to monitor firewall activity alongside other security metrics. Dashboards can be configured to display real-time graphs of blocked threats, geographic maps of connection attempts, and timelines of security incidents. These visual tools make it easier to identify unusual patterns, such as a sudden increase in outbound traffic from a particular subnet or repeated scanning attempts from the same external source. Custom dashboards tailored to specific firewall events can help SOC (Security Operations Center) analysts quickly assess the security posture and take action when necessary.

Automated **alerting and response** mechanisms further increase the value of SIEM integration. When the SIEM detects a pattern of activity that matches a known threat or violates a predefined rule, it can trigger alerts to administrators via email, SMS, or collaboration platforms. In advanced environments, integration with SOAR (Security Orchestration, Automation, and Response) tools enables the system to initiate automatic responses, such as blocking an IP address at the firewall level, disabling a user account, or isolating a suspicious device from the network.

Chapter 5: Threat Intelligence Feeds and Real-Time Updates

Threat intelligence feeds and real-time updates play a central role in modern network defense, especially when integrated with firewalls and other security systems. These feeds provide a continuous stream of up-to-date information about known malicious entities, including IP addresses, domain names, URLs, file hashes, and behavioral indicators associated with malware, threat actors, and ongoing campaigns. The goal of incorporating threat intelligence into security infrastructure is to enable systems to identify, block, and respond to threats as soon as they emerge, rather than relying solely on reactive or manual analysis. As attackers constantly evolve their tactics, techniques, and procedures, having access to current threat data allows organizations to adapt quickly and make informed decisions about what traffic to allow, monitor, or block.

Threat intelligence feeds can originate from a variety of sources, including commercial providers, open-source projects, government agencies, and information-sharing communities such as ISACs (Information Sharing and Analysis Centers). Commercial feeds often include curated, proprietary data gathered from honeypots, global sensor networks, and reverse engineering efforts, offering high-confidence indicators and context-rich metadata. Open-source threat intelligence feeds, while often more limited in scope, still provide valuable data and are widely used due to their accessibility and ease of integration. Some security vendors also offer their own real-time update services, which are integrated directly into their products and automatically enhance the firewall's ability to detect new threats without user intervention.

When a firewall is configured to consume these threat intelligence feeds, it can dynamically update its rule sets or threat databases without requiring manual configuration changes. For example, if a feed reports a newly discovered command-and-control server IP address, the firewall can automatically block any traffic attempting to connect to that address, preventing data exfiltration or malware communication. This type of real-time blocking helps close the gap between threat discovery and threat mitigation, which is critical in reducing the window of exposure during an active attack campaign. Some firewalls allow administrators to create custom policies based on feed categories, such as blocking all IPs flagged for hosting ransomware infrastructure or alerting on outbound requests to phishing domains.

In addition to blocking known threats, threat intelligence feeds also support detection of suspicious activity by providing **contextual enrichment**. For instance, if a user attempts to access a website that is not yet blacklisted but shares characteristics with previously known phishing pages, the firewall can flag the activity for further investigation. This enrichment process allows firewalls to evaluate traffic with more context and assign risk scores or confidence levels to each event. When combined with behavior analysis and historical data, threat intelligence adds a layer of informed decision-making that static rules alone cannot provide.

The effectiveness of real-time threat intelligence depends heavily on the **quality, timeliness, and relevance** of the data. Feeds must be continuously updated to reflect the latest threat landscape, and outdated or inaccurate entries can lead to false positives or missed detections. For this reason, many organizations choose to subscribe to multiple threat intelligence sources and use aggregation platforms that normalize, deduplicate, and prioritize indicators based on reliability and severity. Some advanced firewalls and SIEM systems include built-in threat intelligence management tools that help correlate indicators across multiple feeds, score their credibility, and align them with the organization's specific risk profile or industry sector.

Integration with **security automation** tools further enhances the value of threat intelligence feeds. By feeding indicators into automated workflows, organizations can trigger immediate actions such as isolating affected hosts, updating endpoint detection agents, or launching forensic investigations. This real-time response capability reduces dwell time and helps prevent threats from escalating into full-blown incidents. For example, if a feed flags a new malware hash, the automation system can scan all network traffic and endpoints for the presence of that file, then block execution or quarantine the file if found.

Threat intelligence is not limited to external sources; organizations can also generate **internal threat intelligence** by analyzing their own logs, incidents, and attack patterns. Combining this internal knowledge with external feeds allows for a more tailored and proactive defense strategy. Some firewalls allow for custom threat indicators to be uploaded directly, enabling security teams to block specific threats unique to their environment, such as IP ranges used in past attacks or rogue applications discovered during an internal audit. The constant influx of threat intelligence data, combined with automated updates and contextual analysis, transforms firewalls from static filtering devices into dynamic, adaptive components of a real-time cybersecurity defense system.

Chapter 6: Behavioral Analysis and Anomaly Detection

Behavioral analysis and anomaly detection have become essential techniques in modern cybersecurity, particularly in environments where traditional signature-based detection methods are no longer sufficient to keep up with the speed and sophistication of today's threats. Unlike conventional approaches that rely on known patterns, signatures, or predefined rules, behavioral analysis focuses on observing how users, systems, and applications typically behave under normal conditions and then detecting deviations from these established baselines. These deviations, or anomalies, may indicate the presence of malicious activity, misconfigurations, compromised accounts, or insider threats that would otherwise go unnoticed in environments saturated with encrypted or obfuscated traffic.

Firewalls equipped with behavioral analysis capabilities monitor large volumes of traffic in real time, tracking the frequency, volume, destination, and characteristics of network connections, system processes, login attempts, file transfers, and other operational metrics. Over time, the system learns what is considered normal for a specific device, user, or subnet, and when behavior falls outside those learned parameters, the firewall or associated detection system generates an alert or takes automated action. For example, if a user who typically logs in during business hours from a corporate device suddenly attempts to access critical systems at 3:00 a.m. from a foreign IP address, the anomaly detection engine can flag this activity for further investigation or even trigger an automatic block depending on the configured policy.

One of the key strengths of behavioral analysis is its ability to detect **zero-day attacks** and **fileless malware**, which are often invisible to traditional antivirus tools because they exploit unknown vulnerabilities or live off the land by abusing legitimate processes and services. These types of threats may not generate known indicators of compromise, but they often leave behavioral footprints, such as unexpected privilege escalations, unusual process execution chains, or unauthorized lateral movement within the network. An anomaly-based system does not need to recognize the specific malware to identify the behavior as suspicious, making it an effective line of defense in detecting emerging and evasive attacks.

Behavioral detection also plays a significant role in identifying **insider threats**, whether intentional or accidental. Employees with legitimate access to sensitive systems may begin exfiltrating data, accessing resources outside their job role, or using unauthorized tools, and these behaviors can be subtle and difficult to detect through static rules alone. By continuously learning behavioral baselines for users and systems, anomaly detection engines can spot these deviations, such as a sudden spike in data transfers, repeated access to files previously untouched, or attempts to bypass security controls. In environments where compliance with data protection regulations is critical, such as healthcare, finance, or government sectors, this kind of visibility is essential for preventing data breaches and unauthorized access.

Implementing behavioral analysis involves several components, including data collection, baselining, anomaly detection models, and response mechanisms. Data is typically collected from multiple sources—firewalls, endpoints, identity systems, logs, and network traffic—and centralized for correlation and analysis. The system uses statistical models, machine learning algorithms, or rule-based engines to establish what constitutes normal behavior and then continuously compares real-time data against these baselines. As new data flows in, the models are refined to adapt to changes in user habits, system updates, or organizational growth. This adaptive capability allows the system to remain relevant and accurate over time without requiring constant manual tuning.

False positives can be a challenge in any anomaly detection system, especially during the early stages of deployment when baselines are still being established. To reduce noise and ensure actionable alerts, organizations must fine-tune thresholds, define context-aware policies, and provide feedback to the system when benign anomalies are misclassified as threats. Integration with Security Information and Event Management (SIEM) or Security Orchestration, Automation, and Response (SOAR) platforms can help triage alerts, enrich context, and automate investigative workflows, further increasing the efficiency of security teams.

Behavioral analysis is especially effective when combined with user and entity behavior analytics (UEBA), which expands the scope of detection beyond just network activity to include patterns related to account usage, device behavior, and identity-based access patterns. By correlating behavioral anomalies across multiple layers—

network, user, endpoint, and application—security systems gain a multidimensional view of activity that helps uncover complex threats that would be difficult to identify through isolated events. Through continuous learning, real-time analysis, and contextual awareness, behavioral and anomaly-based detection systems provide a powerful layer of intelligent defense in today's dynamic threat landscape.

Chapter 7: Responding to Security Incidents

Responding to security incidents is a critical function within any organization's cybersecurity operations, requiring swift, coordinated, and methodical action to identify, contain, eradicate, and recover from threats that compromise confidentiality, integrity, or availability. A well-structured incident response begins with **detection and validation**, which often involves alerts generated by firewalls, intrusion prevention systems, endpoint protection tools, SIEM platforms, or user reports. These alerts must be assessed quickly to determine whether they represent genuine threats or false positives. Once a legitimate incident is identified, the next step is **classification and prioritization**, which involves understanding the severity, impact, and scope of the event. This determines the urgency of the response and which resources and personnel need to be involved.

Effective response relies on a predefined **incident response plan (IRP)**, which outlines roles, responsibilities, communication protocols, and decision-making workflows. The incident response team typically includes security analysts, IT personnel, legal advisors, communication staff, and in some cases, external experts or law enforcement agencies. Coordination among these stakeholders is essential, especially in incidents affecting critical infrastructure, customer data, or regulatory compliance. The team must begin by isolating affected systems to prevent the threat from spreading, which may include disabling network interfaces, shutting down servers, revoking user access, or blocking traffic at the firewall. Containment must be carefully managed to avoid disrupting legitimate business functions more than necessary, requiring strong situational awareness and technical expertise.

Forensic investigation plays a major role in understanding the incident. Logs from firewalls, endpoints, authentication systems, and network devices must be collected and analyzed to reconstruct the attack timeline, identify the entry point, and determine what actions the attacker took. Tools like packet analyzers, memory forensics platforms, and file integrity monitoring systems assist in this investigation. The goal is to uncover indicators of compromise (IOCs), such as malicious IP addresses, domain names, file hashes, registry changes, or unauthorized account activity. These indicators help assess the extent of the breach, identify other affected systems, and support the development of specific remediation steps.

Eradication involves removing the threat from all compromised systems. This might mean deleting malware, terminating unauthorized processes, cleaning registry entries, or reinstalling affected software. In more severe cases, systems may need to be rebuilt from trusted backups. During this phase, it is also important to patch vulnerabilities that were exploited during the attack, update firewall rules to block attacker infrastructure, and reset credentials that may have been compromised. Once the threat has been fully eradicated, the organization can move to the **recovery** phase, where systems are restored to normal operation. Recovery must be done carefully and incrementally, with close monitoring for signs of reinfection or residual malicious activity. Any system brought back online should be fully validated to ensure it is clean, secured, and hardened against future attacks.

Communication is another key element of incident response. Internally, stakeholders must be kept informed with accurate and timely updates, while externally, customers, partners, regulators, or media may require communication depending on the nature of the breach. In regulated industries, failure to report incidents within specified timeframes can result in fines or legal consequences. Public messaging must be transparent but controlled, balancing the need for disclosure with the protection of sensitive investigation details.

Once the immediate response is complete, a **post-incident review** should be conducted to evaluate what occurred, how the incident was handled, and what can be improved in the future. This includes reviewing the effectiveness of detection, the speed of containment, the accuracy of classification, and the clarity of communication. Lessons learned should be documented and fed back into the organization's incident response plan, security policies, and training programs. New detection rules may be created based on IOCs discovered during the investigation, and firewalls or other security tools should be updated to prevent recurrence.

Training and simulation exercises help improve the organization's ability to respond to future incidents. Tabletop exercises, red team engagements, and simulated phishing campaigns all contribute to greater preparedness by exposing weaknesses in processes, technologies, or team coordination. When incident response is treated as a continuous improvement cycle rather than a one-time event, organizations can reduce the impact of future breaches, recover faster, and maintain a stronger security posture across the entire infrastructure.

Chapter 8: Automation and Orchestration in Threat Response

Automation and orchestration in threat response have become essential components of modern cybersecurity operations, addressing the challenges posed by increasingly complex attacks, alert fatigue, and the shortage of skilled security professionals. As organizations accumulate vast amounts of data from firewalls, intrusion detection systems, endpoints, identity management platforms, and cloud environments, manually analyzing every event and responding to each potential incident becomes infeasible. Automation introduces the ability to handle repetitive, time-sensitive tasks quickly and consistently, while orchestration coordinates multiple tools, systems, and workflows to operate as a unified defense mechanism. Together, they enable faster response times, reduce the risk of human error, and allow security teams to focus on strategic decision-making rather than being overwhelmed by routine operational tasks.

Threat response automation begins with the ingestion and normalization of data from various sources. Firewalls, for example, generate thousands of events per second related to blocked connections, access violations, protocol anomalies, and application behavior. By feeding this data into a Security Information and Event Management (SIEM) system or a Security Orchestration, Automation, and Response (SOAR) platform, rules can be defined to detect patterns, correlate events across systems, and trigger automated actions. For instance, if multiple failed login attempts are observed from a single IP address, followed by unusual outbound traffic from the same internal host, the automation engine might classify the activity as a brute-force attack or credential compromise and initiate a predefined response workflow.

These workflows can include a variety of automated actions, such as isolating the affected endpoint from the network, blocking the source IP address at the firewall, disabling compromised user credentials, initiating antivirus scans, collecting forensic evidence, and sending alerts to analysts for further investigation. The orchestration layer ensures that these actions are performed in the correct sequence and that communication between systems is smooth and reliable. It also manages dependencies and conditions, such as only executing a containment action if specific criteria are met, or escalating an incident to human analysts if the threat score exceeds a defined threshold.

Automation is also used extensively in **threat intelligence processing**, where raw data from multiple feeds is ingested, deduplicated, enriched with contextual metadata, and applied to firewall rules, web filters, or endpoint protection tools in real time. This enables organizations to respond to new indicators of compromise (IOCs) such as malicious IPs, domains, or file hashes within seconds of detection. Instead of waiting for manual review or ticketing processes, the system can immediately block traffic to newly discovered command-and-control servers or quarantine suspicious files before they can execute. This significantly reduces the dwell time of threats in the network and limits the scope of potential damage.

Automation also supports **incident triage and case management**. When a security event is detected, automated playbooks can gather relevant contextual data from multiple sources— such as user activity logs, network traffic flows, threat intelligence databases, and endpoint telemetry—into a centralized case. The system can then score the severity of the incident, assign it to the appropriate analyst, and track its status through investigation, containment, remediation, and closure. This structured approach ensures consistency in response, improves auditability, and speeds up investigation times by eliminating manual steps.

In more advanced environments, machine learning algorithms are integrated into automation platforms to continuously improve decision-making. These algorithms analyze historical incident data, user behavior, and alert outcomes to refine detection models and recommend optimal responses. For example, if past incidents involving a particular malware family were successfully mitigated by a specific combination of actions, the system can suggest or automatically repeat that strategy when similar behavior is detected again. Over time, this leads to smarter automation and more effective orchestration, as the system learns from experience and adapts to evolving threat landscapes.

Security orchestration also plays a key role in bridging the gap between siloed tools and teams. Many organizations use a wide array of security products from different vendors, each with its own console, configuration language, and event taxonomy. Orchestration platforms integrate these tools through APIs and connectors, creating a centralized interface where automated workflows can span across endpoint protection, firewalls, email security, cloud services, and identity platforms. This integration allows for more cohesive and coordinated threat responses and reduces the time wasted switching between interfaces or re-entering data manually. As automation and orchestration continue to evolve, they serve as force multipliers for security operations centers, enabling organizations to respond with speed, consistency, and precision in an increasingly hostile cyber environment.

Chapter 9: Zero-Day Threats and Evasion Techniques

Zero-day threats and evasion techniques represent some of the most dangerous and difficult challenges in the field of cybersecurity, as they exploit previously unknown vulnerabilities and are specifically designed to bypass traditional defenses such as signature-based detection, antivirus software, and firewalls. A **zero-day vulnerability** refers to a security flaw that has not yet been discovered by the software vendor or security community and therefore has no available patch or fix. A **zero-day exploit** takes advantage of this vulnerability before it becomes publicly known, giving attackers a critical window of opportunity to compromise systems undetected. These threats are especially dangerous because they can affect widely used software and infrastructure, and because no known defense exists at the time of attack, organizations are left exposed until the vulnerability is identified and mitigated.

Attackers leveraging zero-day vulnerabilities often combine them with sophisticated **evasion techniques** to avoid triggering alarms or being caught by automated security systems. One of the most common evasion strategies is **polymorphism**, where the malware constantly changes its code signature each time it is executed or distributed. By altering the appearance of the code, even though the core functionality remains the same, the malware is able to evade signature-based detection systems that rely on matching specific patterns. Similarly, **obfuscation techniques** are used to hide malicious code within legitimate files or disguise it through encryption, compression, or code scrambling, making it harder for static analysis tools to identify the threat.

Another advanced evasion method is **sandbox evasion**, where malware is designed to detect when it is being analyzed in a virtualized or controlled environment and alter its behavior to appear benign. This allows the malware to avoid detection during automated malware analysis and only reveal its malicious payload when it runs in a real user environment. Attackers may introduce delays in execution, require specific user interactions, or check for artifacts associated with sandbox environments such as low memory, absence of user activity, or specific file paths. Once the malware determines it is running in a real environment, it activates its harmful behavior such as data exfiltration, ransomware encryption, or command-and-control (C2) communication.

Living-off-the-land (LotL) techniques are another category of evasion that relies on the abuse of legitimate system tools and processes to carry out malicious actions. Instead of downloading external malware binaries that might be flagged by antivirus or firewalls, attackers use tools like PowerShell, Windows Management Instrumentation (WMI), or scripting engines that are already present on the system. This makes their activities much harder to detect, as they blend into normal system operations and do not create suspicious artifacts. Attackers may use these tools to move laterally, escalate privileges, establish persistence, or communicate covertly with external systems.

In the case of **zero-day threats**, detection becomes a race against time, where defenders must rely on behavioral analysis, heuristic scanning, and anomaly detection to catch early signs of compromise. Instead of matching known patterns, behavioral-based systems analyze how code behaves when executed and look for suspicious patterns such as unauthorized memory access, unusual system calls, or attempts to disable security tools. Firewalls with deep packet inspection and next-generation capabilities may detect anomalies in traffic patterns, such as unexpected protocols being used over common ports or connections to known high-risk IP addresses, even when the specific exploit is unknown.

Attackers also employ **code injection** and **process hollowing**, where malicious code is inserted into legitimate processes to disguise its execution. By hijacking trusted applications like web browsers, system services, or productivity tools, the malware inherits their permissions and avoids detection by appearing to be a safe and authorized process. This allows it to perform malicious activities under the radar of traditional endpoint protection systems. These techniques are frequently used in combination with zero-day exploits to maintain stealth and maximize the attack's effectiveness.

To make detection even more difficult, modern malware often communicates using **encrypted channels**, including HTTPS, DNS tunneling, or custom encrypted protocols. This ensures that even if traffic is intercepted, the contents are not readable without decryption. Since much of internet traffic today is encrypted by default, attackers are able to hide within the noise of legitimate communications, making it critical for firewalls and security systems to support SSL/TLS inspection to analyze encrypted traffic in real time. Attackers may also rotate command-and-control infrastructure frequently or use legitimate services like cloud storage or social media APIs to communicate with compromised hosts, further complicating efforts to block or trace malicious activity.

By combining zero-day exploits with a wide array of sophisticated evasion tactics, attackers can bypass layered defenses, gain unauthorized access, and maintain persistence in networks for extended periods. These threats require organizations to shift from purely reactive strategies to proactive defense models that include continuous monitoring, behavioral analysis, threat intelligence, and rapid patch management to mitigate the impact of unknown and stealthy attacks.

Chapter 10: Building a Proactive Defense Strategy

Building a proactive defense strategy in cybersecurity involves anticipating threats before they occur, minimizing attack surfaces, and continuously adapting to an evolving threat landscape rather than reacting only after incidents happen. A proactive approach begins with **threat modeling**, where organizations identify their most valuable assets, understand potential adversaries, and evaluate how those adversaries might attempt to compromise systems. This process helps define the priorities of the security program and directs resources toward the protection of the most critical components of the infrastructure. By understanding the tactics, techniques, and procedures (TTPs) of likely attackers, security teams can develop countermeasures that address specific risks rather than applying generic controls.

One of the core components of proactive defense is **network segmentation**, which involves dividing the network into distinct zones with tightly controlled communication paths between them. This limits lateral movement for attackers who gain a foothold in the environment and isolates critical systems, making it harder for threats to spread undetected. Firewalls, access control lists, and internal traffic monitoring are used to enforce these boundaries, ensuring that only approved communications occur between segments. Additionally, **least privilege access** should be enforced across systems, users, and services, allowing entities only the minimum level of access necessary to perform their functions. This reduces the potential impact of compromised accounts or misconfigured systems.

Continuous monitoring and visibility are fundamental to proactive defense, requiring the deployment of logging, telemetry, and analytics across endpoints, servers, network devices, and cloud infrastructure. This data should be collected in real-time and analyzed using tools such as SIEM (Security Information and Event Management) platforms, which can correlate events, detect anomalies, and trigger alerts for suspicious activity. To reduce alert fatigue and prioritize genuine threats, organizations should implement **behavioral analytics** and **user and entity behavior analytics (UEBA)**, which focus on deviations from established baselines rather than relying solely on static signatures. Monitoring should also include encrypted traffic inspection to identify threats hidden in SSL/TLS sessions and to ensure policy compliance.

Another essential component of proactive defense is the integration of **threat intelligence** into security operations. Consuming real-time feeds from reputable sources allows organizations to identify emerging threats, track indicators of compromise (IOCs), and automatically update firewall and endpoint protection rules to block malicious IP addresses, domains, or file hashes. Threat intelligence also supports **attack surface management**, where security teams continuously scan their environments for exposed services, unpatched systems, or misconfigurations that could be exploited by adversaries. By discovering and remediating vulnerabilities before they are targeted, organizations reduce their risk profile and disrupt attackers' opportunities for exploitation.

Security awareness training contributes significantly to a proactive defense posture by empowering users to recognize and respond appropriately to social engineering, phishing attempts, and unusual behavior. Humans are often the weakest link in cybersecurity, and regular education programs can dramatically reduce the likelihood of successful attacks that depend on user interaction. These training sessions should be supplemented with simulated phishing campaigns, incident response drills, and feedback loops to reinforce learning and identify areas for improvement.

Automation also plays a vital role in proactive defense by enabling faster detection and response. Using **Security Orchestration, Automation, and Response (SOAR)** platforms, organizations can define workflows that automatically contain threats, collect forensic data, isolate systems, and notify stakeholders without requiring manual intervention. This improves consistency, reduces response time, and frees analysts to focus on higher-value tasks. Automation is particularly effective when used in conjunction with **vulnerability management**, where newly discovered threats trigger automated scans, patch verifications, or configuration audits to ensure that defenses remain current and aligned with best practices.

Regular **penetration testing** and **red teaming exercises** are also key elements of a proactive defense strategy. These assessments simulate real-world attack scenarios to test the effectiveness of existing controls and identify weaknesses that may have been overlooked. Findings from these exercises feed directly into continuous improvement efforts, allowing security teams to close gaps and improve response procedures. Coupled with **security baselining and**

hardening guides, organizations can ensure that systems are configured securely from the outset and remain resilient against exploitation. Proactive defense requires a cultural shift within the organization, where security is treated as an ongoing process rather than a one-time deployment, and where agility, visibility, and accountability drive every decision made in the pursuit of protecting digital assets.

BOOK 4
NEXT-GEN FIREWALLS AND THE FUTURE OF
NETWORK DEFENSE: AI, ZERO TRUST, AND
EMERGING TECHNOLOGIES IN CYBERSECURITY

ROB BOTWRIGHT

Chapter 1: What Makes a Firewall "Next-Gen"?

What makes a firewall "next-gen" is its ability to go beyond traditional packet filtering and port blocking by incorporating deep inspection, application awareness, identity-based controls, and integrated threat prevention features into a single, unified platform. Traditional firewalls, often referred to as first- or second-generation firewalls, primarily operated at layers 3 and 4 of the OSI model and made decisions based on source and destination IP addresses, ports, and protocols. While this approach was effective in early network environments, it became inadequate as applications started using dynamic ports, encrypted communications, and techniques that allowed them to bypass basic filtering rules. A next-generation firewall (NGFW), in contrast, adds intelligence, flexibility, and context to the decision-making process, allowing it to understand not just where traffic is going but what it is and who is generating it.

One of the defining features of a next-gen firewall is **application awareness and control**. Rather than relying solely on port numbers, NGFWs use deep packet inspection (DPI) and pattern recognition to identify specific applications within network traffic, even if they are using non-standard ports or encrypted channels. This enables administrators to write policies that allow or block traffic based on application identity rather than just protocol, which is especially important in environments where productivity, security, and compliance are tightly regulated. For example, a company might want to allow access to Microsoft Teams for collaboration but block access to unauthorized file-sharing platforms or social media applications, all of which may use the same underlying ports or encryption.

Next-generation firewalls also support **user and identity awareness**, allowing policy enforcement based on user roles, group memberships, or specific individuals rather than just IP addresses. This integration is typically achieved by connecting the firewall to an identity provider such as Active Directory, LDAP, or a cloud-based identity service. With this capability, a rule can be written to permit database access only for users in the finance department or to block file transfers for guest users, regardless of the device or IP address being used. Identity-based controls support the principle of least privilege and help enforce security policies that align more closely with business roles and responsibilities.

Another major component that sets NGFWs apart is **integrated threat prevention**. These firewalls are equipped with built-in intrusion prevention systems (IPS), antivirus engines, anti-malware scanning, and

URL filtering to detect and block known threats before they can reach internal systems. Unlike traditional firewalls, which often had to rely on external devices for advanced inspection, NGFWs combine these features within a single platform, reducing latency and improving operational efficiency. Threat prevention in NGFWs is not limited to signature-based detection; many also include heuristic analysis and behavioral inspection to identify unknown or zero-day threats based on suspicious activity patterns.

Next-gen firewalls also offer **SSL/TLS inspection**, allowing them to decrypt, inspect, and re-encrypt encrypted traffic. With the majority of modern internet traffic now encrypted by default, this capability is critical for detecting threats that are otherwise hidden in secure sessions, such as malware delivered through HTTPS or command-and-control traffic disguised as legitimate web browsing. SSL inspection requires careful configuration to balance security with privacy and performance, and NGFWs often provide granular controls to exclude certain types of traffic or trusted destinations from decryption when appropriate.

Centralized management and automation are also important features of NGFWs, particularly in large or distributed environments. These firewalls often support cloud-based or centralized consoles where policies, logs, alerts, and software updates can be managed across multiple devices and locations. This centralized visibility allows for better correlation of events and more efficient response to threats. Automation capabilities such as dynamic policy updates based on threat intelligence feeds, auto-remediation of infected hosts, or integration with Security Orchestration, Automation, and Response (SOAR) platforms further enhance the firewall's ability to adapt to real-time threats.

Next-generation firewalls are also designed to support **cloud and hybrid architectures**, offering virtualized versions that can be deployed in public cloud environments such as AWS, Azure, or Google Cloud. These virtual firewalls extend consistent security policies to cloud workloads and enable inspection of east-west traffic between cloud-native applications. NGFWs are also built with scalability in mind, supporting high-throughput environments, encrypted traffic loads, and multi-gigabit performance without compromising inspection depth or latency. By incorporating these capabilities, NGFWs provide a more holistic, intelligent, and adaptive security layer that aligns with the needs of modern networks and threat landscapes.

Chapter 2: Application Control and Layer 7 Inspection

Application control and Layer 7 inspection are vital features of modern firewalls and network security systems, offering visibility and enforcement at the application layer of the OSI model rather than relying solely on IP addresses, ports, and protocols. Traditional firewalls operated at Layers 3 and 4, using packet headers to make access decisions based on source and destination IP addresses, port numbers, and protocol types. While this method was effective in the early days of networking, it is no longer sufficient in environments where applications dynamically use non-standard ports, encryption, and evasive techniques to bypass basic filtering mechanisms. Application control introduces the ability to identify, monitor, and control individual applications regardless of the transport mechanisms they use, while Layer 7 inspection provides the deep analysis needed to interpret and classify that traffic accurately.

Layer 7, also known as the application layer, is where user-facing services operate, including web browsers, file transfers, messaging platforms, streaming services, and enterprise applications.

Applications at this layer often share common ports and can disguise their traffic to appear benign. For instance, a file-sharing application might use TCP port 443, which is also used by secure web traffic, making it indistinguishable from legitimate HTTPS traffic to a traditional firewall. With Layer 7 inspection, the firewall goes beyond the transport layer and analyzes the actual payload of the traffic, identifying the specific application, its behavior, and sometimes even the individual features being used, such as video streaming versus file uploading in a collaboration tool.

Application control enables administrators to define policies that allow, block, throttle, or log specific applications based on business needs. These policies can be based on the application itself, its category, user identity, time of day, or traffic volume. For example, an organization may choose to allow Microsoft Teams for internal collaboration but block Zoom or Slack for external communication to maintain control over data flow and compliance. Similarly, video streaming sites such as YouTube may be allowed during lunch hours but restricted during working hours to conserve bandwidth and maintain productivity. Layer 7 inspection makes this possible by continuously analyzing traffic to detect application signatures, protocol behaviors, and usage patterns, even if the application attempts to evade detection by using encryption, tunneling, or obfuscation.

Modern firewalls and security gateways use a combination of **deep packet inspection**, **heuristic analysis**, and **machine learning models** to identify applications operating at Layer 7. These methods look at various attributes of the traffic, including HTTP headers, TLS handshake details, DNS queries, and behavioral patterns over time. This allows for more precise identification, especially in cases where applications are not static or predictable. Application signatures are regularly updated by vendors to keep up with emerging services, changes in behavior, or newly developed evasion tactics. The combination of static and dynamic detection methods ensures a high degree of accuracy while minimizing false positives.

Layer 7 inspection also enables **granular enforcement** within applications. Instead of simply allowing or blocking an entire application, security policies can control specific functions within that application. For example, an organization might allow Dropbox for file viewing and synchronization but block file uploads or sharing links. In webmail services, users might be allowed to read emails but restricted from sending attachments or accessing external links. This level of control helps organizations balance productivity and security by allowing legitimate use of tools while preventing risky or unauthorized behavior.

Another advantage of application control and Layer 7 inspection is the ability to generate **detailed analytics and reporting**. Administrators can view real-time dashboards that show top-used applications, bandwidth consumption by application, application usage by user or department, and trends over time. This visibility provides insights that are critical for capacity planning, compliance audits, and risk assessments. In regulated industries, being able to prove that sensitive data is not being transferred through unauthorized applications or services is an essential part of maintaining trust and meeting legal obligations.

Application control also supports integration with identity and access management systems, allowing enforcement of policies not just by IP address but by **user identity** or group membership. This integration ensures that only authorized users can access specific applications, regardless of where they connect from or which device they use. Combined with Layer 7 inspection, it provides a context-aware framework for security, where traffic is evaluated based on what the application is, who is using it, how it is being used, and whether that usage aligns with the organization's security policies and business objectives. This intelligent, layered approach is essential for managing modern network environments where cloud services, mobile access, and encrypted applications are the norm.

Chapter 3: Integrating Firewalls with Zero Trust Architectures

Integrating firewalls with Zero Trust architectures involves rethinking traditional network security assumptions and aligning firewall capabilities with the core principles of Zero Trust, where no device, user, or application is inherently trusted, even if it resides inside the corporate network. Zero Trust is built on the foundation of continuous verification, least-privilege access, segmentation, and contextual policy enforcement, and firewalls play a key role in enforcing these controls across network boundaries, internal segments, and cloud environments. Traditional perimeter-based models treated everything inside the network as trusted by default, which created opportunities for lateral movement and privilege escalation once a threat actor bypassed the initial defenses. In a Zero Trust model, firewalls must evolve from being gatekeepers at the edge to becoming distributed enforcement points throughout the entire environment.

The integration begins with the deployment of firewalls in strategic positions where they can inspect and control both north-south and east-west traffic. North-south traffic refers to communications between internal systems and external entities, such as internet access or cloud service usage, while east-west traffic involves internal communications between systems, applications, and users. Zero Trust emphasizes tight control over east-west traffic to limit the ability of threats to propagate laterally within the network. Next-generation firewalls with application awareness, identity integration, and microsegmentation capabilities are ideal for this role, as they can enforce policies based on user identity, device posture, application context, and data sensitivity rather than just IP addresses or ports.

To support Zero Trust principles, firewalls must integrate with identity providers such as Active Directory, LDAP, SAML, or modern identity-as-a-service platforms. This integration allows security policies to be enforced based on who the user is, what role they have, and whether they have passed strong authentication checks such as multi-factor authentication. Instead of allowing access based solely on network location, the firewall uses contextual identity information to determine whether a user should be allowed to connect to a specific resource. For example, access to a financial database might only be granted to members of the finance team using managed devices from approved locations and during business hours, with all these conditions enforced at the firewall level through identity-aware policies.

Firewalls in a Zero Trust architecture also play a key role in **microsegmentation**, which involves dividing the network into smaller zones and enforcing granular policies for communication between them. Each zone can represent a business unit, application tier, or sensitivity level, and the firewall ensures that only explicitly authorized traffic flows between them. This segmentation reduces the attack surface, limits the blast radius of any potential breach, and simplifies compliance by aligning network boundaries with data governance requirements. Microsegmentation is often implemented using virtual firewalls in cloud and hybrid environments, where traditional hardware appliances are not practical.

Continuous monitoring and policy adaptation are essential for Zero Trust, and firewalls must be integrated with systems that provide real-time telemetry, threat intelligence, and behavioral analysis. By collecting logs and metadata from firewall activity and correlating them in Security Information and Event Management (SIEM) or Extended Detection and Response (XDR) platforms, security teams gain visibility into traffic patterns, policy violations, and potential threats. When an anomaly is detected—such as a user accessing unfamiliar resources or a spike in internal data transfers—the firewall can dynamically update policies or trigger automated response actions through integration with Security Orchestration, Automation, and Response (SOAR) platforms.

In addition to on-premises enforcement, Zero Trust architectures require consistent policy enforcement in cloud-native and remote work environments. Firewalls that support **cloud integration** and **zero trust network access (ZTNA)** can extend the same identity-based, context-aware policies to users and applications regardless of their physical location. This is particularly important in a world where users work from various locations and devices, often bypassing traditional network perimeters. Cloud-delivered firewalls and secure access service edge (SASE) frameworks further enhance this capability by delivering firewall functions as a service, ensuring scalability and policy consistency across distributed networks.

The successful integration of firewalls into a Zero Trust framework depends on their ability to interoperate with other security systems, continuously verify access conditions, and enforce least-privilege policies in real time. Firewalls must become part of an adaptive security fabric where access decisions are informed by identity, device posture, application behavior, and threat intelligence, and where every connection is evaluated before it is allowed, regardless of origin or destination. By doing so, firewalls help operationalize Zero Trust principles and transform static, perimeter-based security into a dynamic, context-driven model that aligns with modern IT infrastructure and threat landscapes.

Chapter 4: Identity-Based Access and User-Aware Policies

Identity-based access and user-aware policies are foundational to modern network security, especially in dynamic environments where users access resources from multiple locations, devices, and networks. Traditional security models focused primarily on IP addresses, ports, and protocols, assuming that if a device was inside the network perimeter, it could be trusted. However, this assumption no longer holds true in a world shaped by mobile workforces, bring-your-own-device policies, and cloud-hosted services. Identity-based access shifts the focus from where traffic originates to who is generating it, allowing security policies to be tailored based on user roles, group memberships, authentication methods, and even behavioral context.

Firewalls and security systems that support identity-based access integrate with directory services such as Active Directory, LDAP, or cloud-based identity providers like Azure AD, Okta, or Google Workspace. This integration allows security administrators to apply access control rules not just to devices or IP addresses, but directly to users and groups. For example, rather than allowing all traffic from a specific subnet to access internal databases, an identity-based policy might permit only members of the finance department to initiate connections to a financial database, regardless of their location or device. This type of granular control helps enforce the principle of least privilege by ensuring users only have access to the resources necessary for their job functions.

User-aware policies also provide flexibility to define security conditions based on additional context, such as time of day, geographic location, device posture, or authentication strength. A user accessing a resource during normal business hours from a corporate laptop on a trusted network might be granted full access, while the same user attempting to access that resource from a personal device in an unrecognized location may be subject to restrictions, step-up authentication, or even complete denial of access. These policies adapt dynamically to changing risk conditions, enhancing both security and usability.

Another benefit of identity-based access is the ability to enforce application-specific policies that consider both the user and the application in question. For example, a policy can be created to allow marketing employees to use social media tools like LinkedIn and Twitter but block access to productivity-draining platforms like TikTok or online games. Application-layer controls integrated with identity awareness ensure that these policies are enforced regardless of how the applications are accessed, including via web browsers, mobile apps, or desktop clients. This control is especially useful in environments where encrypted traffic and cloud services are common, as it allows for visibility and enforcement even when traditional port-based methods fall short.

Identity-based policies are also crucial in enabling secure remote access. With the rise of hybrid work environments, organizations must ensure that users accessing internal systems remotely are properly authenticated and authorized. Firewalls and secure access solutions can apply identity-based policies that restrict access to certain services or resources based on user roles, while still allowing full productivity. For instance, IT administrators may be allowed to use remote desktop tools and VPN tunnels, whereas regular users are limited to accessing approved SaaS applications through a secure browser portal.

In environments where compliance is important, such as healthcare, finance, or government, identity-based policies help enforce regulations by tightly controlling who can access sensitive data and under what conditions. Auditing and reporting features that track user access and activity provide the necessary documentation for compliance reviews and investigations. By logging user-based access attempts rather than just IP-based events, organizations gain clearer insight into user behavior, enabling better anomaly detection and faster response to insider threats or compromised credentials.

The integration of identity with access control also supports collaboration across distributed teams and partner organizations. Temporary users, contractors, or third-party vendors can be granted time-limited access to specific systems or applications without exposing the entire network. These access rights can be automatically revoked once the engagement ends, and policies can be applied that limit their ability to transfer data, install software, or change configurations. This ensures that access remains tightly controlled while still enabling business operations to move forward efficiently.

User-aware firewalls and security systems must also support multi-factor authentication, federated identity, and integration with modern identity and access management (IAM) systems to provide secure and seamless experiences. The combination of identity, behavior, and contextual awareness enables precise policy enforcement that adapts to real-world conditions and helps organizations maintain strong security without introducing unnecessary friction for users. Through identity-based access, security becomes not just a barrier but a strategic enabler of secure productivity.

Chapter 5: Machine Learning and AI in Threat Detection

Machine learning and artificial intelligence are transforming threat detection by enabling security systems to move beyond static rules and signatures and instead make dynamic, data-driven decisions that adapt to evolving threats. Traditional security solutions rely heavily on predefined patterns of known attacks, which are effective for catching repeat offenders but struggle when faced with zero-day exploits, novel malware strains, or sophisticated attacks that modify their behavior to avoid detection. Machine learning allows systems to identify patterns, correlations, and anomalies within massive volumes of network and system data that would be impossible for human analysts or static filters to process in real time. By continuously learning from data, these models improve over time, adapting to new threats and refining their ability to distinguish between normal and malicious behavior.

Machine learning in threat detection typically begins with data collection and feature extraction, where raw data such as logs, traffic flows, endpoint telemetry, file metadata, and user behavior are ingested and analyzed. Features are specific attributes extracted from this data that serve as inputs for machine learning models—for example, the frequency of login attempts, file access times, destination ports, domain reputations, or deviations from historical baselines. Supervised learning models are trained using labeled datasets that include examples of both benign and malicious activity, allowing them to learn what indicators are commonly associated with real threats. Unsupervised learning models, by contrast, are designed to detect anomalies by identifying data points that deviate from established norms, making them well suited for discovering unknown or emerging threats.

In network security, machine learning is used to detect threats such as port scanning, lateral movement, exfiltration attempts, botnet activity, and command-and-control communications. These threats often operate within traffic that appears legitimate on the surface, especially when encrypted. By analyzing patterns in traffic volume, session length, timing intervals, or destination behavior, machine learning models can flag suspicious sessions even if the content of the traffic cannot be directly inspected. In email security, machine learning is used to detect phishing attempts by analyzing message structure, sender reputation, URL behavior, and writing style. In endpoint protection, models detect malware by analyzing code structure, API calls, runtime behavior, and memory usage rather than relying on specific file hashes.

AI systems can also combine multiple machine learning models in a layered or ensemble approach, improving overall accuracy by correlating outputs from different models and reducing the likelihood of false positives or negatives. For example, one model may specialize in detecting anomalies in user behavior, while another focuses on unusual network traffic, and a third monitors file integrity or system calls. When these models work together, the security platform gains a more comprehensive understanding of what constitutes a threat, enabling more confident and accurate detection. This fusion of behavioral analytics across multiple data domains is especially valuable for identifying multi-stage attacks, where each individual stage may appear harmless but the sequence reveals malicious intent.

Threat detection systems powered by AI can also prioritize alerts based on severity and contextual awareness, reducing alert fatigue for human analysts. Instead of flooding security operations centers with thousands of low-confidence alerts, AI can rank incidents by risk level, suggest probable causes, and even recommend specific actions. This allows analysts to focus on high-impact threats and respond more efficiently. Some systems go a step further by enabling automated responses through integration with security orchestration platforms, where machine learning models not only detect threats but trigger actions such as isolating devices, blocking IPs, revoking credentials, or launching forensic scans.

Continuous training is a key aspect of using machine learning in security. As threats evolve, models must be updated with new data to remain effective. This can involve retraining supervised models with newly labeled datasets or fine-tuning unsupervised models to adapt to changing network behavior. Feedback loops from analysts, such as marking alerts as true or false positives, are valuable in improving model performance over time. Organizations must also be aware of adversarial techniques, where attackers attempt to deceive AI models by injecting noise, evading detection patterns, or mimicking legitimate behavior. Defensive AI must therefore be designed to recognize adversarial signals, incorporate explainability, and be validated against realistic attack scenarios to ensure robust detection in complex and high-stakes environments.

Chapter 6: Cloud Firewalls and Security-as-a-Service (SECaaS)

Cloud firewalls and Security-as-a-Service (SECaaS) are key components of modern cybersecurity strategies, particularly as organizations increasingly migrate workloads, applications, and infrastructure to public, private, and hybrid cloud environments. Traditional firewalls, designed to protect on-premises networks with fixed perimeters, are no longer sufficient in today's decentralized and highly dynamic architectures. Cloud firewalls extend the concept of perimeter security into the cloud by providing scalable, flexible, and centralized security controls that can be applied across distributed environments. These firewalls are either native to cloud platforms, such as AWS Network Firewall, Azure Firewall, or Google Cloud Armor, or provided by third-party vendors as virtual appliances or software-defined firewalls that can be deployed and managed in cloud infrastructure.

Unlike physical firewalls that require hardware appliances and manual setup, cloud firewalls are deployed as virtual instances and can be spun up quickly using automation tools or cloud orchestration templates. They can inspect traffic flowing between cloud workloads (east-west traffic) as well as traffic entering or leaving the cloud (north-south traffic). Cloud firewalls support the same capabilities as their on-premises counterparts, such as access control, packet filtering, application awareness, and threat detection, but they are specifically optimized for cloud scalability, API integration, and multi-tenant architectures. They are often tightly integrated with the cloud provider's identity and access management systems, logging services, and monitoring tools, allowing for seamless policy enforcement and centralized visibility.

Security-as-a-Service (SECaaS) takes this model even further by delivering firewall functionality and other security services as cloud-native solutions managed entirely by external providers. These services may include next-generation firewalls, intrusion prevention systems, web filtering, data loss prevention, email security, endpoint protection, and identity management, all offered through subscription-based models. SECaaS allows organizations to offload the complexity of managing and maintaining security infrastructure while gaining access to the latest threat intelligence, automated updates, and 24/7 monitoring capabilities. It is particularly beneficial for small to medium-sized businesses that lack dedicated security teams or data center infrastructure, as well as for large enterprises seeking to scale security across global environments without adding operational overhead.

One of the key advantages of cloud firewalls and SECaaS platforms is **elastic scalability**, allowing security resources to grow or shrink automatically based on demand. As traffic increases due to application spikes, remote user access, or geographic expansion, cloud-based firewalls can adjust capacity without the need for hardware upgrades or manual intervention. This agility ensures that performance remains consistent even under heavy load and that security policies remain effective regardless of infrastructure changes. Policies and configurations can be centrally managed and deployed across multiple regions or cloud providers, supporting hybrid and multi-cloud strategies without requiring separate toolsets for each environment.

Cloud firewalls and SECaaS also support **zero trust principles**, enforcing identity-aware policies that require continuous authentication and authorization before granting access to resources. By integrating with federated identity providers and context-aware access controls, these services help implement the least-privilege model at scale. For example, traffic between microservices can be controlled based on the identity of the service, the security posture of the instance, or the risk profile of the user initiating the request. These attributes are evaluated dynamically to determine whether the connection should be allowed, monitored, or blocked.

Visibility is another important benefit of cloud firewalls and SECaaS, as they offer detailed logging, telemetry, and analytics dashboards to help organizations understand traffic patterns, detect anomalies, and respond to incidents. Many platforms provide integrations with Security Information and Event Management (SIEM) systems and Security Orchestration, Automation, and Response (SOAR) tools, enabling security teams to automate threat detection and response workflows. Alerts from cloud firewalls can trigger automated remediation steps, such as isolating workloads, revoking access, or launching forensics processes, thereby reducing mean time to respond (MTTR) and limiting the impact of attacks.

As threats become more sophisticated and environments become more complex, cloud firewalls and Security-as-a-Service models offer a flexible, cost-effective, and forward-looking solution for securing assets and data wherever they reside. They align with the principles of cloud-native architecture, DevSecOps, and continuous compliance, making them essential for securing modern, scalable, and agile IT infrastructures.

Chapter 7: Securing Hybrid and Multi-Cloud Environments

Securing hybrid and multi-cloud environments presents unique challenges and requires a carefully coordinated strategy that addresses the complexities of managing security across different platforms, networks, and administrative boundaries. A hybrid environment combines on-premises infrastructure with public or private cloud services, while a multi-cloud environment uses services from multiple cloud providers such as AWS, Microsoft Azure, and Google Cloud Platform. These setups offer flexibility, scalability, and redundancy but introduce risks related to inconsistent security controls, lack of visibility, fragmented identity management, and diverse compliance requirements. As organizations distribute workloads and data across these environments, it becomes essential to implement a unified security posture that spans all infrastructures while adapting to the specific tools and capabilities of each provider.

One of the first steps in securing a hybrid or multi-cloud setup is establishing **consistent identity and access management** across all environments. Relying on isolated user databases or siloed access policies can lead to configuration drift and unauthorized access. Integrating cloud identity providers with centralized directories such as Active Directory or using federated identity systems enables the application of unified access policies based on user roles, device health, authentication strength, and location. Implementing single sign-on (SSO) and multi-factor authentication (MFA) ensures that only authorized users can access critical resources, regardless of where those resources are hosted. Role-based access control (RBAC) must be strictly enforced to minimize the privileges granted to users and services in each cloud environment.

Network segmentation and traffic control are critical components in reducing the attack surface across hybrid and multi-cloud architectures. Organizations should define and enforce security zones for various workloads, departments, or sensitivity levels and use firewalls, access control lists, and software-defined perimeters to regulate traffic between them. In a hybrid cloud scenario, secure connectivity between on-premises data centers and cloud environments is typically achieved through virtual private networks (VPNs) or dedicated links like AWS Direct Connect or Azure ExpressRoute. Traffic that flows between cloud regions or between different cloud providers must also be inspected and controlled using cloud-native firewalls or third-party network security appliances deployed in the cloud. These tools must support Layer 7 inspection, identity-based policies, and threat intelligence integration to detect and block suspicious activity across all segments.

Maintaining **visibility and monitoring** across all cloud platforms is another essential part of the strategy. Each cloud provider offers its own logging, telemetry, and monitoring services, such as AWS CloudTrail, Azure Monitor, and Google Cloud Logging. However, relying on these tools in isolation can create visibility gaps and hinder incident response efforts. Aggregating logs and metrics from all platforms into a centralized Security Information and Event Management (SIEM) system allows for correlation, analysis, and alerting based on unified data. This centralization enables security teams to detect cross-platform threats, monitor policy compliance, and investigate incidents with full context. Integrating these tools with Security Orchestration, Automation, and Response (SOAR) systems further enhances response capabilities by automating repetitive tasks and initiating real-time countermeasures.

Data protection and encryption must also be a top priority in hybrid and multi-cloud deployments. Data should be encrypted at rest and in transit using strong, consistent encryption standards across all platforms. Key management can be handled through cloud-native key management services (KMS) or external hardware security modules (HSMs) that provide centralized control over cryptographic keys. Organizations should classify their data based on sensitivity and apply data loss prevention (DLP) policies that restrict unauthorized sharing or movement of data between environments. Cloud storage services must be configured to prevent public access by default, and data access should be logged and monitored to detect abnormal usage patterns.

To reduce misconfigurations—a leading cause of cloud security breaches—organizations should adopt **infrastructure as code (IaC)** practices and use automated tools for security posture management. Tools like AWS Config, Azure Security Center, and third-party cloud security posture management (CSPM) platforms can continuously scan cloud environments for deviations from baseline configurations, exposed services, or unused access rights. Security checks can be integrated into the development pipeline through DevSecOps practices, ensuring that security policies are applied before infrastructure is deployed. These tools provide real-time alerts and remediation guidance, helping teams maintain continuous compliance with internal policies and external regulations.

Successfully securing hybrid and multi-cloud environments requires a shift from traditional perimeter-based security models to a more distributed, identity-aware, and automated approach that treats every environment as potentially hostile while maintaining centralized visibility, policy enforcement, and governance.

Chapter 8: The Role of SASE and Edge Security

The role of SASE and edge security has become increasingly important in modern network architecture as organizations adapt to a landscape shaped by cloud computing, remote work, and decentralized infrastructure. SASE, which stands for Secure Access Service Edge, is a cloud-native framework that combines network and security functions into a single, unified service delivered from the cloud. It merges technologies such as software-defined wide area networking (SD-WAN), secure web gateways, cloud access security brokers (CASB), zero trust network access (ZTNA), and firewall-as-a-service (FWaaS) to create a cohesive solution that secures access to resources regardless of where users, devices, or applications are located. Traditional models that relied on centralized data centers and perimeter-based security controls are no longer effective in this distributed environment, and SASE addresses this by bringing security and connectivity closer to the users and devices at the network edge.

Edge security refers to the protection of data, applications, and users at or near the point where they interact with the network, whether that be a branch office, remote location, IoT device, or mobile user. In the SASE model, edge security is embedded into the access layer, meaning that users are authenticated, authorized, and their traffic inspected before it ever reaches the core network or cloud application. This is achieved through a globally distributed network of points of presence (PoPs), where security enforcement is applied as close to the user as possible, reducing latency and improving performance while maintaining consistent security policy enforcement. This shift allows organizations to provide secure access without backhauling traffic to centralized data centers, which not only adds delay but also increases complexity and cost.

One of the core components of SASE is Zero Trust Network Access, which enforces strict access controls based on identity, device posture, location, and other contextual factors. Instead of trusting users or devices simply because they are connected to a corporate network, ZTNA ensures that every request is evaluated dynamically and granted access only to specific resources for which the user is explicitly authorized. This aligns with the principle of least privilege and helps to prevent lateral movement within the network in the event of a breach. In the context of SASE, ZTNA is integrated directly into the edge, enabling real-time access decisions and seamless enforcement of identity-aware policies.

Another key element of SASE is Firewall-as-a-Service, which extends next-generation firewall capabilities into the cloud. FWaaS includes features such as application control, intrusion prevention, URL filtering, and DNS security, all delivered from the SASE edge infrastructure. This eliminates the need for on-premises firewall appliances at each branch or remote site, reducing the hardware footprint and simplifying management. Because the firewall policies are defined centrally and enforced at the edge, organizations can maintain consistent security across all locations while allowing traffic to flow directly to cloud services or the internet without sacrificing visibility or control.

Cloud Access Security Broker functionality within SASE enables the monitoring and control of data and user interactions with cloud-based applications, providing visibility into shadow IT, enforcing compliance with corporate policies, and protecting against data leakage. CASBs can apply granular policies such as blocking the upload of sensitive data to unauthorized services or requiring encryption for certain types of content. In a SASE model, CASB capabilities are integrated into the edge, ensuring that cloud access is governed consistently regardless of whether users are working from a corporate office, a remote location, or a mobile device.

Secure Web Gateway features in SASE filter web traffic for malicious content, enforce acceptable use policies, and block access to known malicious domains. This inspection happens in real time at the edge, leveraging global threat intelligence feeds to protect users against phishing, malware, and other internet-based threats. The integration of these features into a unified SASE platform allows for better visibility, faster response times, and simplified policy management across diverse environments.

By consolidating multiple security functions into a single cloud-native service, SASE simplifies architecture, reduces operational overhead, and provides scalable protection that adapts to the needs of modern organizations. Edge security, as delivered through SASE, ensures that wherever users connect from and whatever resources they access, security is consistent, intelligent, and tightly aligned with business policies. This model is especially effective in supporting digital transformation, enabling remote work, securing multi-cloud deployments, and reducing risk across an increasingly complex and distributed IT landscape.

Chapter 9: Compliance, Privacy, and Regulatory Integration

Compliance, privacy, and regulatory integration have become fundamental pillars of modern cybersecurity strategies, especially as organizations operate across multiple jurisdictions with varying legal obligations and heightened scrutiny around data protection practices. In this landscape, firewalls and security infrastructure must not only defend against technical threats but also ensure that security controls align with the requirements set forth by laws such as the General Data Protection Regulation (GDPR), the Health Insurance Portability and Accountability Act (HIPAA), the California Consumer Privacy Act (CCPA), the Payment Card Industry Data Security Standard (PCI DSS), and other sector-specific or region-specific frameworks. The ability to integrate compliance and privacy controls directly into firewall policies and logging mechanisms helps organizations demonstrate accountability, minimize legal risk, and build trust with customers and regulators.

One of the key requirements across most regulatory frameworks is the protection of personally identifiable information (PII) and sensitive data, such as financial records, health information, or customer credentials. Firewalls must be capable of identifying and controlling traffic that involves sensitive data, ensuring that it is encrypted, not transmitted to unauthorized destinations, and only accessed by authorized users. Features such as deep packet inspection, application control, and content filtering enable firewalls to enforce policies that prevent the unintentional or malicious transmission of protected data. For example, a firewall can block outbound traffic that contains social security numbers or credit card numbers when such transfers are not compliant with organizational data handling policies.

Logging and auditing are essential components of regulatory integration, as most frameworks require detailed records of access attempts, policy changes, data transfers, and security events. Firewalls must generate logs that are timestamped, tamper-evident, and stored in accordance with data retention requirements defined by applicable laws. These logs must be integrated with centralized Security Information and Event Management (SIEM) systems to support real-time monitoring, forensic investigations, and periodic compliance audits. Additionally, organizations must ensure that access to logs is restricted and auditable, allowing only designated personnel to review or export sensitive security data. This capability is crucial for demonstrating compliance during audits and for identifying anomalies that may indicate a breach or policy violation.

Privacy laws such as GDPR and CCPA also introduce obligations related to **data minimization**, **data sovereignty**, and **user consent**. In a security context, this means that systems must be designed to collect only the data necessary for security operations, store it in compliant geographic regions, and ensure that personal data is not used for purposes beyond its intended scope. Firewalls configured with privacy-aware policies can enforce geographic restrictions on data flows, blocking traffic to or from jurisdictions that lack adequate data protection regulations or that violate contractual data residency agreements. They can also prevent unauthorized scanning or data collection by inspecting outbound requests and controlling access to web applications and APIs.

Another area where compliance and security intersect is **incident response and breach notification**, which are legal requirements under many data protection laws. Firewalls play a role in early detection of unauthorized access, data exfiltration attempts, or suspicious traffic that could signal a breach. By integrating firewall alerts with incident response platforms, organizations can ensure that potential breaches are rapidly contained and that the necessary notifications are issued within mandated timeframes, such as the 72-

hour window defined by GDPR. Automated triggers can be set up to alert compliance teams, initiate forensic data collection, and generate reports detailing the nature of the breach, the data affected, and the remediation steps taken.

Firewalls also support compliance by enabling **role-based access control (RBAC)** and enforcing **least privilege** principles. Regulatory frameworks emphasize that only authorized personnel should have access to sensitive systems and data, and that these permissions should be narrowly defined. Firewalls integrated with identity management systems can enforce policies that restrict administrative access to security systems, limit remote access to approved users, and prevent lateral movement within internal networks. These measures help maintain segregation of duties and reduce the risk of insider threats or accidental exposure.

Compliance, privacy, and regulatory integration require that firewalls not only act as enforcement points for security policies but also as active components of a larger governance framework. By aligning technical capabilities with legal and regulatory obligations, firewalls contribute to both the protection of data and the accountability mechanisms that ensure organizations are meeting their compliance responsibilities.

Chapter 10: The Future of Firewalls in a Post-Perimeter World

The future of firewalls in a post-perimeter world is being shaped by the rapid evolution of IT infrastructures, where cloud computing, remote work, mobile devices, and edge computing have dismantled the traditional concept of a well-defined network boundary. In this decentralized environment, the role of firewalls is no longer limited to guarding a physical perimeter but must instead extend protection to users, devices, applications, and data wherever they reside. As organizations adopt hybrid and multi-cloud architectures, implement software-as-a-service platforms, and support globally distributed workforces, firewalls must become more adaptive, context-aware, and deeply integrated into broader security frameworks that emphasize identity, behavior, and policy rather than location. Traditional firewalls relied on inspecting traffic that crossed a clear ingress or egress point between trusted internal networks and the untrusted internet, using rules based on IP addresses, ports, and protocols. In a post-perimeter world, this model is insufficient because many users now access applications directly from unmanaged networks, devices regularly operate outside corporate boundaries, and data resides in cloud environments far from the original network. To address these shifts, firewalls are transforming into cloud-native, distributed security services that function as policy enforcement points embedded into every layer of connectivity. This includes cloud firewalls deployed in virtual environments, firewall-as-a-service platforms integrated with secure access service edge (SASE) frameworks, and micro-segmentation firewalls enforcing workload-level protections inside data centers and cloud platforms.

Next-generation firewalls are evolving to focus less on network location and more on identity, context, and application behavior. This shift enables firewalls to make decisions based on who the user is, what device they are using, what application they are accessing, where they are located, and the current risk posture. These capabilities require integration with identity providers, endpoint detection and response tools, and threat intelligence feeds to enforce policies that adapt in real time. For example, access to sensitive resources can be allowed for a user logged in from a managed corporate device on a trusted network, but restricted or denied if that same user connects from a personal device over public Wi-Fi. Firewalls that support this level of granularity are essential for implementing zero trust architectures, where continuous verification is required and trust is never assumed based on network presence alone.

Firewalls in the future will also rely more heavily on artificial intelligence and machine learning to detect and respond to threats in real time. These technologies allow firewalls to analyze vast amounts of data, detect patterns of anomalous behavior, and make decisions faster than human operators. For instance, if a normally quiet server suddenly begins transmitting large amounts of data to an unfamiliar external destination, machine learning algorithms can flag this as potential data exfiltration and trigger automated containment measures through the firewall. As cyber threats grow in sophistication and volume, AI-driven analytics and autonomous response capabilities will become a standard feature in firewall solutions, reducing dwell time and improving response efficiency across all layers of the network.

Integration with broader ecosystems is another key aspect of the firewall's future. In the post-perimeter world, security cannot operate in silos. Firewalls must exchange data and collaborate with other components such as cloud workload protection platforms, endpoint security solutions, SIEMs, SOAR systems, and vulnerability management tools. APIs and cloud-native orchestration frameworks allow firewalls to participate in automated security workflows, where policy changes, threat intelligence updates, and response actions are synchronized across the environment. This integration helps enforce consistent security controls regardless of where the user or application is located, providing a unified security posture across disparate platforms and services.

Scalability and performance are also driving innovation in firewall design, with solutions now capable of handling encrypted traffic inspection at scale, managing massive volumes of east-west cloud traffic, and maintaining low latency while applying complex rulesets. As more traffic becomes encrypted by default, firewalls must support inline decryption, inspection, and re-encryption without degrading user experience or violating privacy policies. Distributed decryption points and selective inspection based on risk assessment will help balance performance with security in environments where high throughput and real-time access are critical.

In a post-perimeter world, firewalls are becoming less of a physical barrier and more of a distributed policy enforcement layer that follows users, devices, and data wherever they go. Their function is not limited to stopping traffic at the edge but includes enabling secure access, maintaining visibility, and enforcing adaptive policies throughout a dynamic and borderless digital ecosystem. Firewalls are no longer just appliances; they are evolving into a ubiquitous security presence embedded in every layer of connectivity, helping organizations maintain control and protect assets in an increasingly decentralized and cloud-driven world.

Conclusion

As the digital landscape continues to evolve, so too must the tools and strategies we use to protect it. Across these four volumes—*Foundations of Firewall Technology, Firewall Configuration and Deployment, Advanced Threat Detection and Response*, and *Next-Gen Firewalls and the Future of Network Defense*—we've explored the essential building blocks, operational best practices, advanced integration methods, and forward-looking innovations that define the modern firewall.

From the origins of packet filtering and core networking protocols to the complexities of deep packet inspection, machine learning, Zero Trust, and cloud-native security models, this series has aimed to equip engineers, architects, and security professionals with the technical knowledge and strategic insight needed to design, deploy, and manage effective firewall solutions in any environment.

Firewalls are no longer static gatekeepers at the network perimeter—they have become dynamic, intelligent, and context-aware enforcement points woven into every layer of the infrastructure. Whether you're securing a single branch office, protecting workloads across a multi-cloud environment, or enabling secure access for a remote global workforce, the firewall remains a critical component of a layered defense strategy.

As threats become more sophisticated and infrastructures more distributed, the responsibility of engineers is not just to deploy technology, but to understand it deeply, adapt it intelligently, and integrate it responsibly. The future of cybersecurity depends on professionals who can bridge theory and application, policy and performance, and innovation and resilience.

This guide has provided the framework. The next step is yours to take—armed with knowledge, grounded in best practices, and ready to meet the challenges of a connected world.